THE VOICE OF THE EAGLE

ox spualis aqui
le auditū pulſat ęcctę·
exterior ſenſuſ·tranſe-
untē accipiat ſonitū·
Jnterior animuſ·ma -
nentē penetret intelle-
ctum ·Uox altiūdi uolantiſ·ñ aerē cor-
poreū·uel ethera·uel totiuſ ſenſibiliſmun-
di habitū ſupuolantiſ·Sed omnē theóriā·
ultra omīa quę ſunt·et quę ñ ſunt·citiuo-
liſ intime theológie penniſ·clariſſime
ſupéq? contēplationiſ obtitib? tranſcen-
dentiſ·Dico autē quę ſunt.quę ſiue hu-
manū·ſiue angticū·non omīno effugi-
unt ſenſum·Quę uero ñ ſunt·quę ꝑ fe-
cto omíſ intelligentię uireſ relinquunt·

Manuscript page of the opening of the *Homily.*
Courtesy of the British Museum (Harley 7183).

THE VOICE OF THE EAGLE

*Homily on the Prologue
to the Gospel of St. John*

JOHN SCOTUS ERIUGENA

Translated with an Introduction and Reflections

by Christopher Bamford

LINDISFARNE PRESS

Published by Lindisfarne Press
RR4, Box 94 A-1,
Hudson, New York 12534

Library of Congress Cataloging-in-Publication Data

Erigena, Johannes Scotus, ca. 810-ca. 877
  [Homilia in prologum Sancti Evangeli secundum Joannem. English]
  The voice of the eagle: the heart of Celtic Christianity: John Scotus Eriugena's
Homily on the prologue to the Gospel of St. John/translated, with an introduction and
reflections by Christopher Bamford.
  Translation of: Homilia in prologum Sancti Evangelii secundum Joannem.
  Includes bibliographical references.
  ISBN 0-940262-36-3
  1. Bible. N.T. John I, 1-18 — Early works to 1800.   2. Sermons, Latin
—Translation into — Early works to 1800.   3. Sermons, English — Translations
from Latin — Early works to 1800.   4. Catholoic Church — Sermons — Early works
to 1800.   5. Celtic Church — Sermons — Early works to 1800.   I. Bamford,
Christopher.   II. Title.

BS2615.4.E7513   1990
226.5'07—dc20   90-49163
                                                                         CIP

Published in Europe by Floris Books
15 Harrison Gardens, Edinburgh, Great Britain
British Library CIP Data available
ISBN 0-86315-516-2

In the USA
ISBN 0-940262-36-3

Table of Contents

Introduction

The greatest Christian theologians, such as John
Scotus Eriugena and Thomas Aquinas, never opposed
the teachings of Plato to Christianity, but —
especially in the case of Eriugena — they recognized
that a specific inner struggle was the foundation upon
which metaphysical concepts could guide the transformation of human nature.... These theologians
offer a form of philosophy which we might call
contemplative metaphysics, a form of inner empiri-
cism in which ideas about the inner universe are
studied and experienced in one's own inner world.

Jacob Needleman (1980)

John Scotus Eriugena was Irish, Irish-born, as his names suggest
— "Scotus, the Scot or Irishman"; "Eriugena, the Irish-born"
— and he must have been educated in Ireland, or at least in the
Celtic tradition, as the range of his learning attests. For he knew
Greek, a smattering of Hebrew, and was fully perfected in the
Seven Liberal Arts — "the Seven Gifts of the Holy Spirit," as
Alcuin calls them. This is to say that he was a master of the
Trivium of Grammar, Rhetoric, and Logic, and of the Quadriv-
ium of the sacred sciences of Arithmetic, Geometry, Music, and
Astronomy. In addition to such "professional" accomplishments,
Eriugena brought with him from the monastery schools of the
Celtic Church — thought by many to be the highest level of
spiritual culture ever attained by Christianity — a deep, power-
ful, and lived knowledge of Christian life and theology. Eriugena
himself, however, was neither monk nor priest: he was a
layman, a lover of wisdom, a holy sage: the *sanctus sophista
Johannes* ("the holy sage John") according to his epitaph. "A

wonderful man he must have been," in the words of Samuel
Taylor Coleridge.

Eriugena was born early in the ninth century, for by 850–1
C.E. he was already in France, a scholar of repute attached to the
Cathedral School of Laon, and well known to King Charles the
Bald. We first hear of him in connection with a controversy
surrounding the so-called Augustinian doctrine of double predestination — the doctrine that held that all human beings were
predestined by God to either salvation or damnation — a
doctrine which Eriugena termed "a most cruel and stupid
madness."

The issue of predestination had been raised by a monk,
Gottschalk, the son of a Saxon noble, who had been placed in
the monastery of Fulda against his will and vowed to a religious
life by his father. Gottschalk rebelled against this cruel fate — to
no avail. Condemned to monkish life, he plunged himself into
the study of St. Augustine where, to his delight, he discovered
the doctrine of double predestination. "The theory he developed in this seclusion," writes R.L. Poole, "had a natural affinity
with the morbid cravings, the vindictive passions of a disap-
pointed man. It assuaged his regrets for lost earthly life by the
confidence of eternal happiness hereafter. It gave him a weapon
with which to assail his opponents: their reward was already
decided for them. He pressed the certainty of their doom with
fanatical violence. . . ."

In this mood Gottschalk stirred up a wasp's nest of
controversy. The various participants hurled Augustinian texts
at each other without discrimination until Augustine's thought,
like his authority, was thoroughly undermined. Finally, Hincmar
of Rheims, Gottschalk's leading opponent, asked Eriugena to
give his opinion.

With Eriugena's entry into the fray, theological casuistry
became deep theosophical argument. Eriugena began by claim-
ing that true religion and true philosophy were one and the
same. Hence a religious problem was a philosophical problem

— an unusual position at any time and one fraught with radical consequences. For since true philosophy rested in the unity of God, the only reality, who is good by definition and for whom it is not one thing to be and another to will, but for whom being and willing are the same, there could only be a single predestination, that to eternal salvation. But even this, however, was for Eriugena only a manner of speaking, for predestination invokes time — and double predestination, duality — neither of which are realities for God. For God, therefore, suffering, sin, and evil do not exist and so cannot be predestined. God knows only what is real. He does not know what occurs as a result of ignorance. On the human plane the law of cause and effect obtains; indeed, here it is the rule. As sin arises from the individual will, so does punishment. For Eriugena, neither sin nor punishment comes from God himself, but only from the sinner, whose sin will continue to punish itself until at the end of time all nature will be restored. The essential nature of the sinner, however, is not involved in this, since every nature in its essence is divine. What sins, what is evil, is somehow overlaid. Indeed, if evil is real, it is only real insofar as it contains an effort toward the good, which alone is real. Nor, finally, since the universe is one, could there be any place of perpetual punishment. All things proceed from the good and in the good they must end. The only hell is ignorance.

For such opinions Eriugena was censured and his work condemned by the Synod of Valence (855) as *Pultes Scottorum*, "Scot's Porridge." But his supremacy of spirit could not be denied. Therefore he was asked by Charles the Bald to translate from the Greek the works of the great mystical theologian Dionysius the Areopagite, thought to be identical both with the disciple of St. Paul and with St. Denis, the patron saint of France. Eriugena completed this work of translation — which was to be so important for the development of later medieval culture — except for a Commentary on *The Celestial Hierarchies* added later — in 860. The translations of Dionysius were followed by others of St. Gregory of Nyssa and St. Maximus the Confessor. By virtue of these, according to Gilson, our Celtic sage came to write in Latin but to think in Greek. As I.P. Sheldon Williams writes in the *Cambridge History of Later Greek and Early Medieval Philosophy*, "Thus [Eriugena] fortuitously became acquainted with three of the most characteristic and important documents of the Greek Christian Platonism; the effect of their influence upon him was to bring him as wholly into the Greek tradition as if he had been a Byzantine writing in Greek, and to make of him the agent through whom the Western world came into this valuable inheritance." This is true. We have the impression that in Eriugena, "the final accomplishment of ancient thought" according to Henry Bett, as in a time capsule, the entire wisdom of the Platonic world is made secure in Christianity and left as an inheritance for the future benefit of Western culture. And yet we also find in Eriugena a distinctive flavor, a unique framework at once cosmic and ecological, that does not exist in quite the same powerfully embodied (incarnational) form elsewhere. This we can only assume was part of his Celtic background and inheritance.

By the time he was engaged on these translations, Eriugena was probably already composing his major work, the *Periphyseon* or *On the Division of Nature*. This astounding synthesis of theology, philosophy, cosmology and anthropology (these last being the same for Eriugena) represents a perfect, nondualistic fusion of Christianity and Platonism and constitutes the only philosophical alternative in the West to the Aristotelian scholasticism of St. Thomas Aquinas. Two points only need be made to indicate the significance of Eriugena's thought. First, he makes no opposition between being and consciousness or consciousness and nature. These are complementaries within a single unity, poles of a unique process whose ground is divine consciousness as knowledge and whose existence is divine procession through hierarchy and participation. Second, the threefold human being of body, soul, and spirit is primary. As the center of, and mediator between, heaven and earth, visible and invisible, the human being for Eriugena is the place where — the means or organ by which — the entire universe may be united and transfigured and God known in his own self-knowing.

Such premises, though necessary for our times of cultural transformation and ecological awareness, were dangerous to a Church striving to hold an unsophisticated population in social and political cohesion. Groups of freethinking, pantheistic and otherwise heretical mystics — such as the Amaurians, Cathars, and Brethren of the Free Spirit — sought confirmation of their various doctrines in the *Periphyseon*:

" 'sunt lumina' said the Oirishman to King Carolus, 'OMNIA,
all things that are are lights'
and they dug him up out of sepulture
soi disantly looking for Manichaeans."

(Ezra Pound, Canto LXXIV)

The result was that in 1225 Eriugena's work was condemned by a papal bull. Luckily, however, this was not before its influence had worked mightily in the rebirth of the "symbolic" mentality of the Twelfth Century Renaissance, both in the School of Chartres and among the Cistercians and Victorines.

In addition to the works already mentioned, Eriugena also wrote a lost *Treatise on the Eucharist*, a *Commentary* on Martianus Capella's *Marriage of Philology and Mercury* — a key work in the transmission of the wisdom of the Seven Liberal Arts — some poems, and — of course — the *Homily on the Prologue to the Gospel of St. John* and an unfinished *Commentary on the Gospel of St. John*.

Composed toward the end of his life (865–70), Eriugena's *Homily* ("The Voice of the Eagle") — "one of the greatest homilies of medieval spiritual literature" (Moran) — is a lyrical, polished and metaphysically precise meditation on the first

seventeen verses of St. John's Gospel. A homily being a sermon
or short discourse intended to be inserted into the liturgy, *The
Voice of the Eagle* was clearly written for the Third or Day Mass
on Christmas Day, when the Prologue to St. John's Gospel was
read. The many manuscripts — Benedictine and Cistercian
— attest to its popularity during the Middle Ages when, however, it was only rarely attributed to Eriugena. Of fifty-four
manuscripts examined by Jeauneau, only five are attributed to
Eriugena. Of the rest, eleven are anonymous, thirty are attributed to Origen, seven to Chrysostom, and one to St. Gregory
Nazianzen.

Though intended for religious use, the *Homily* is no minor
work. It is, on the contrary, the mature masterwork of a
philosopher-poet of the first order. Some critics, indeed, like the
German scholar Huber, have seen in it the most perfect of
Eriugena's works. Others have felt, when reading it, that they
were reading a chapter from the *Periphyseon*. As Edouard
Jeauneau, the text's editor, wrote, "The author is no simple
rhetorician. He is a thinker, one of the most profound and subtle
of the Middle Ages. And this thinker is as wholly present in his
Homily, as he is in his *Periphyseon*." Jeauneau goes on to say
that the *Homily*, as it were, completes and resumes a triptych
— begun with the *Commentary* on Dionysius' *Celestial Hierarchies* and continued with the *Periphyseon* — in which Eriugena's
entire, poetic, spiritual universe of light unfolds, each part
recapitulating and containing the whole under a different
aspect.

The aspect from and of which the *Homily* speaks is of
course the theological. The divine, cosmic, and human functions of the Word or *Logos* in the beginning are here presented
in the form of a profound epistemological meditation on the
meaning and end of creation. In twenty-three short chapters,
Eriugena manages to digest and transform the classical heritage
of Pythagoras and Plato, and to unite these with the Hebraic and

prophetic vision of a Living God, so as to present a message of Christian *gnosis*, unique in its significance for our time.

The translator's "Reflections," which make up the second half of the book, attempt to unpack some of the life-giving meaning contained in Eriugena's luminous sentences. These reflections, distilled from a much larger work, were inspired both by a personal search for the meaning of Christianity and by the sense that the continuity of Western culture depended upon taking seriously such epochal thinkers as Johannes Scotus Eriugena. The project was begun at a time when similarly serious studies of great thinkers in other religious traditions were being widely undertaken. Western Sufis were dedicating themselves to the works of Ibn Arabi, Buddhists were studying Nagarjuna and Dogen, Vedantists were reading Sankara: it seemed necessary to accord the same life-and-death meaning to the study of a Western cultural figure. Who better than Eriugena, termed by Thomas Whittaker, "probably inferior to no metaphysician that ever lived"? Eriugena came to mind above all for two related reasons. His work was both epistemological and cosmological. This meant that it was both accessible to contemporary consciousness — which is scientific and seeks a way of knowing — and provided a spiritual and philosophical foundation for thinking ecologically about the world we live in. Add to this the fact that, alone among Western philosophers, Eriugena provides a cosmology that is Hermetic and so permits the understanding of those proto-ecologists of the imagination, the Alchemists, and you have an irresistible challenge — a call the translator could not refuse.

* * *

Some time after 877, while working on his *Commentary on the Gospel of St. John*, Eriugena died. According to William of Malmesbury, he had come to end his days in England, teaching at the Abbey of Malmesbury, where his students stabbed him to death with their pens. After his death, his body lay in the Church of St. Laurence, until a heavenly light advised the monks to bury the scholar in the Great Church, to the left of the altar.

As John O'Meara wrote, "While the spirit of Plato, the Neoplatonists, and the mystics lives on, his ideas will not die." Eriugena's influence has been seen in the Kabbalistic Zohar of Moses de Leon, in Grosseteste, Eckhart, Tauler, Ruysbroeck and the German Mystics, in Nicholas of Cusa, Spinoza, and Giordano Bruno, in Hegel, Solovyov and even Ezra Pound who, in Hugh Kenner's words, "fetched, via Fenellosa's notes, transcendentalism from China, and made Kung out of hints from Scotus Eriugena."

ACKNOWLEDGMENTS

I have been graced with friendship, love, and support in innumerable ways. To this community of family, friends, colleagues, and neighbors I offer grateful thanks. Bless you all.

CHRISTOPHER BAMFORD

Christopher Bamford is co-director of both The Lindisfarne Press and The Anthroposophic Press. He is the author of numerous articles and the co-editor of the book, Celtic Christianity: Ecology and Holiness.

The
Prologue
to the Gospel
of St. John

The Prologue
to the Gospel of St. John
(King James Version)

1. In the beginning was the Word, and the Word was with God, and the Word was God.

2. The same was in the beginning with God.

3. All things were made by him; and without him was not any thing made that was made.

4. In him was life; and the life was the light of men.

5. And the light shineth in darkness; and the darkness comprehended it not.

6. There was a man sent from God, whose name was John.

7. The same came for a witness, to bear witness of the Light, that all men through him might believe.

8. He was not that Light, but was sent to bear witness of that Light.

9. That was the true Light, which lighteth every man that cometh into the world.

10. He was in the world, and the world was made by him, and the world knew him not.

11. He came unto his own, and his own received him not.

12. But as many as received him, to them gave he power to become the sons of God, even to them that believe on his name:

13. Which were born, not of blood, nor of the will of the flesh, nor of the will of man, but of God.

14. And the Word was made flesh, and dwelt among us, (and we beheld his glory, the glory as of the only begotten of the Father,) full of grace and truth.

15. John bare witness of him, and cried, saying, This was he of whom I spake, He that cometh after me is preferred before me: for he was before me.

16. And of his fulness have all we received, and grace for grace.

17. For the law was given by Moses, but grace and truth came by Jesus Christ.

Homily
on the Prologue
to the Gospel of St. John

I

The Voice of the Eagle

The voice of the spiritual eagle strikes in the hearing of the church. May our outer senses grasp its transient sounds, may our inner spirit penetrate its enduring meaning.

This is the voice of the bird of high flight — not of the bird who soars above the material air or over the aether, orbiting the entire sensible world — but the voice of that spiritual bird who, on swiftest wings of innermost theology and intuitions of most brilliant and high contemplation, transcends all vision and flies beyond all things that are and are not.

By the things that are, I mean the things that do not wholly escape perception, either angelic or human, since they come after God and because of their numbers do not transcend what has been fashioned by the single cause of all. And by the things which truly are not, I mean those which actually surpass the powers of all understanding.

The blessed theologian John therefore flies beyond not only what may be thought and spoken, but also beyond all mind and meaning. Exalted by the ineffable flight of his spirit beyond all things, he enters into the very arcanum of the one principle of all. There he clearly distinguishes the superessential unity and the supersubstantial difference of the beginning and the Word — that is, of the Father and the Son — both incomprehensible, and begins his Gospel saying: "In the beginning was the Word."

II

O blessed John

O blessed John, not unworthily are you called John. The name John is Hebrew. Translated into Greek, this name means "to whom is given." For to whom among theologians is given what is given to you? Namely, to penetrate the hidden mysteries of the highest good and to intimate to human mind and senses what was there revealed and declared unto you. To whom else, I pray, was given grace so great and of such a kind?

Perhaps some will say such a grace was given to the chief of the Apostles, I mean to Peter, who, when the Lord asked him whom he thought he was, replied, "Thou art the Christ, the Son of the living God." However it may be said without fear, I think, that Peter in answering thus spoke more as the figure of faith and action than that of knowledge and contemplation.

Why? For the obvious reason that Peter is always presented as the model of faith and action, while John portrays the type of contemplation and knowledge. The one indeed leans on the bosom of the Lord, which is the sacrament of contemplation, while the other often hesitates, which is the symbol of restless action.

For the execution of divine commands, before it becomes habitual, may shatter the pure brilliance of virtue and fall short in its judgements, clouded by the fog of sense-bound thinking. The keenness of profoundest contemplation, on the other hand, once it has perceived the countenance of the truth, neither hesitates, nor slips, nor is ever darkened by any cloud.

III

Both however run

Both Apostles, however, run to the tomb.

Christ's tomb is Holy Scripture, in which the mysteries of his divinity and humanity are secured by the weight of the letter, just as the tomb is secured by the stone.

But John runs ahead and arrives before Peter — for contemplation, being deeply purified, penetrates more sharply and speedily into the secret power of the divine intent than does action, which still needs purification.

Nevertheless — although they have both run to the tomb and both enter into it — Peter enters first, and John only enters after him. For if Peter symbolizes faith, then John signifies the intellect. Therefore, since it is written, "Unless you believe you will not understand," faith necessarily enters first into the tomb of Holy Scripture, followed by the intellect, for which faith has prepared the entry.

Peter, who recognized the Christ, now made human and divine in time, and said, "You are the Christ, the Son of the living God," flew very high, but higher still flew the one who, having known this same Christ as God, born of God before time, said, "In the beginning was the Word."

Let it not be thought, however, that we prefer John to Peter. For who could do so? Who indeed among the Apostles could be higher than he who is, and is called, their chief?

We do not prefer John to Peter, we only compare action and contemplation — the soul, still needing purification, to the soul that is already purified. We only compare virtue that is still in the process of ascending to an immutable state to virtue that has already attained it. We do not here consider the personal dignity of the Apostles, but only investigate the beautiful distinctions that are made in the divine mysteries.

Thus Peter, action practicing virtue, perceives, through the virtue of faith and action, the Son of God confined in the flesh in a wonderful and ineffable manner. But John, who is the highest contemplation of the truth, wonders at the Word of God in itself, before the flesh, in its principle or absolute and infinite origin — that is, in the Father.

Peter, truly, when he observes eternity and time made one in Christ, is led by divine revelation; but it is John alone who leads the faithful among souls to knowledge of what in Christ is eternal.

IV

The spiritual bird

The spiritual bird therefore, fast-flying, God-seeing — I mean John, the theologian — ascends beyond all visible and invisible creation, passes through all thought and intellect, and, deified, enters into God who deifies him.

O Blessed Paul, you were caught up, as you yourself assert, into the third heaven, to paradise; but you were not caught up beyond every heaven and every paradise. John, however, went beyond every heaven formed and paradise created, beyond every human and angelic nature.

In the third heaven, O vessel of election and teacher of the gentiles, you heard words not lawful for a human being to utter. But John, the observer of the inmost truth, in the paradise of paradises, in the very cause of all, heard the one Word through which all things are made.

It was permitted to him to speak this Word, and to proclaim it, as far as it may be proclaimed, to human beings. Therefore most confidently he cried out, "In the beginning was the Word."

V

John therefore

John, therefore, was not a human being but more than a human being when he flew above himself and all things which are. Transported by the ineffable power of wisdom and by purest keenness of mind, he entered into that which is beyond all things — namely, into the secret of the single essence in three substances and the three substances in the single essence.

He would not have been able to ascend into God if he had not first become God. For, as the gaze of our eyes cannot feel the forms and colors of sensible things unless it is first mixed and united with the sun's rays, so the souls of saints cannot receive the pure knowledge of spiritual things transcending all intelligence, unless they have first been made worthy of participation in the incomprehensible truth.

Thus the holy theologian, transmuted into God, and participating in the truth, proclaims that God, the Word, subsists in God, the beginning: that is, that God, the Son, subsists in God, the Father. "In the beginning," he says, "was the Word."

Behold heaven opened and the mystery of the highest and holiest Trinity revealed! Observe the divine angel ascend above the son of man, proclaiming him to be the Word existing in the beginning before all things. Observe him descend upon the same son of man and cry, "And the Word was made flesh."

The angel descends when the Gospel speaks of the Word made human supernaturally among all things from the Virgin. The angel ascends when the Gospel proclaims this same Word born superessentially from the Father before and beyond all things.

VI

In the beginning

"In the beginning was the Word," he writes.

Here we must note that the significance that the holy Evangelist gives to this utterance "was" is not temporal but substantial. For the verb "to be," whence we derive by irregular conjugation the imperfect "was," contains a double meaning. Sometimes it means the subsistence, without temporal movement, of whatever is predicated, in which case it is called "the substantial verb." At other times, however, it indicates like other verbs a temporal movement. Therefore, when the Evangelist affirms that "In the beginning was the Word," it is as if he were openly saying, "In the Father subsists the Son." What person, indeed, of sound mind would say that the Son at any time subsisted temporally in the Father? For only where eternity is known may immutable truth be understood.

And lest anyone think that the Word subsists in the beginning without substantial difference, the Evangelist immediately adds, "And the Word was with God." That is to say, "The Son subsists with the Father in unity of essence and distinction of substance."

And again, lest a venomous contagion infect anyone — such as that the Word is only in the Father and with God, but does not subsist substantially and co-essentially as God with the Father — which error befell the faithless Arians — the Evangelist immediately adds, "And the Word was God."

Similarly, knowing that there would not lack those who would claim that he was not referring to one and the same Word when he said "In the beginning was the Word" and "the Word was God," and would assert that the "Word in the beginning" and "The Word was God" were different — in order to destroy this heretical view — the Evangelist adds next, "This was in the beginning with God."

That is to say: the Word, which is God with God, is not other than He who was in the Beginning.

This may be grasped more meaningfully in the Greek versions of the Gospel. In these, it says *autos*, that is, "the same," which may refer to either God or to the Word — for these two words, *Theos* and *Logos* ("God" and "Word") are masculine in Greek, as indeed is *autos* also. And therefore the statement "And the Word was God, this (same) was in the beginning with God" may be understood to state more clearly than if it had been said in broad daylight "This God-Word, who is with God, is the same of whom I say, 'In the beginning was the Word.' "

VII

All things were made through him

All things were made through him. Through God-the-Word himself, through the very God-Word, all things were made.

And what does "All things were made through him" mean if not that as the Word was born before all things from the Father, all things were made with him and by him? For the generation of the Word from the Father is the very creation itself of all causes, together with the operation and effect of all that proceeds from them in kinds and species. Truly, all things were made from the generation of God-the-Word from God-the-beginning.

Hear, then, the divine and ineffable paradox — the un-openable secret, the invisible depth, the incomprehensible mystery! Through him, who was not made but begotten, all things were made but not begotten.

The beginning, the principle, from whom all things are is the Father; the beginning, the principle, through whom all things exist is the Son. The Father speaks his Word — the Father brings forth his Wisdom — and all things are made. The prophet said, "In wisdom has thou made them all." And elsewhere, introducing the Father in person, the Father says, "My heart has brought forth." And what did his heart bring forth? He explains it himself: "I spoke a good Word." I speak a good Word, I bring forth a good Son. The Father's heart is his own substance, of which the Son's own substance was begotten.

The Father precedes the Son, not naturally, but causally. Hear the Son himself say, "My father is greater than I." That is to say: "His substance is the cause of my substance." Causally, I say, the Father precedes the Son; naturally, the Son precedes all things which are made through him. The substance of those things, which are made by him, began in him before all the ages of the world, not in time but with times. Time, indeed, is made with all things that are made. It is neither made before them, nor is it preferable to them, but it is co-created with them.

VIII

The consequence of the Word

And what is the consequence of the Word which was spoken from the mouth of the most high? Certainly the Father did not speak in vain, neither fruitlessly nor without great effect, since even human beings, speaking among themselves, effect something in the ears of their hearers. Three things, therefore, we must believe and understand: the Father speaking, the Word proclaimed, and the things effected by the Word. The Father spoke, the Word was begotten, and all things were effected. Hear the prophet speak: "For he spake and it was done." That is: He brought forth his Word, by whom all things were made.

And lest you hold that among those things which are, some were made by the very Word of God himself, while others in fact were made, or existed, outside of him — so that the things which are and are not are referable to a single principle — the Evangelist adds to all his previous theology the conclusion: "And without him was not anything made that was made." That is: nothing was made without him, because he himself circumscribes and comprehends all, and nothing can be conceived that is co-eternal, consubstantial, or co-essential with him, except the Father and the Spirit that proceeds from the Father through the Word.

This is easier understood in Greek. For where the Latin says *sine ipso* (without him), the Greek says *choris autou*, that is, outside him. And similarly the Lord himself says to his disciples: "Without me you can do nothing." "You," he says, "who without me have not been able to make yourselves, what can you do without me?" Here again the Greek says not *aneu* but *choris*, that is, not "without" but "outside."

For this reason, therefore, I say that the Greek is more easily understood, because one who hears *sine ipso* can still think "without his help or counsel," thereby attributing to him neither the totality nor all things. Understanding *extra* as "outside," however, nothing whatsoever is left that is not made in and through him.

IX

What was made in him

"What was made in him was life." At the furthest distance from all reason and intellect, the blessed Evangelist reveals the divine mysteries. He shows the God-Word clearly revealed in the God who speaks, leaving behind for those who contemplate the Divine Scriptures the revelation of the Holy Spirit in both.

Indeed, just as whoever speaks, in the word that he speaks, necessarily breathes forth breath, so God the Father, together and at the same time, gives birth to his Son, and through his Son, thus born, produces his Spirit.

Following this, the Evangelist adds that through the Son all things were made and that nothing subsisted outside of him.

Then, as if to pursue the unfolding of his theology from another beginning, he says, "What was made in him was life." Earlier he had said, "All things were made by him," and then, as though someone had asked him about these things which are made by God — how and what these things made by him were in him — the Evangelist replies, "What was made in him was life."

This last sentence is ambiguous and may be spoken in two ways. For either one says, "What was made," adding, "in him was life." Or one says, "What was made in him," and then adds, "was life."

Through these two punctuations, two different meanings are given to us for contemplation. For the contemplation which asserts, "What was made in places, discrete times, kinds, forms, and distinct numbers, whether of sensible or intellectual substance, compact or separated, all this was life in him," is not the same as the one which declares, "What was made in him is not other than life."

Let our meaning therefore be the following: All things which are made in him, in him are life and are one. All things were — subsist — in him as causes before they are in themselves as effects. For the things that are made through him are beneath him in one way; and the things that he is are in him in another.

X

All things

All things, therefore, which were made by the Word, live in him unchangeably and are life. In him all things exist neither by temporal intervals or places, nor as what is to come; but all are one in him, above all times and places, and subsist in him eternally.

Visible, invisible, corporeal, incorporeal, rational, irrational — heaven and earth, the abyss, and whatever is therein — in him all live and are life and subsist eternally. Even what seems to us to be without all vital movement lives in the Word.

And if you want to know how, or by what reason, all things which are made through the Word thus subsist vitally, causally, and in the same manner in him, consider examples chosen from created nature. Learn to know the maker from those things which are made in him and by him. "For the invisible things of him," as the Apostle says, "are clearly understood by the intelligence, being understood from the things which are made."

See how the causes of all things which this spherical, sensible world contains subsist simultaneously and similarly in that sun which alone is called the great luminary of the world. Thence the forms of all bodies proceed; thence the beauty and diversity of colors; and whatever else may be known of sensible nature.

Consider the infinite, multiple power of the seed — how many grasses, fruits, and animals are contained in each kind of seed; and how there surges forth from each a beautiful, innumerable multiplicity of forms. Contemplate with your inner eye how in a master the many laws of an art or science are one; how they live in the spirit that disposes them. Contemplate how an infinite number of lines may subsist in a single point, and other similar examples drawn from nature.

From the contemplation of such as these, raised above all things by the wings of natural contemplation, illuminated and supported by divine grace, you will be able to penetrate by the keenness of your mind the secrets of the Word and, to the extent that it is granted to the human being who seeks signs of his God, you will see how all things made by the Word live in the Word and are life: "For in him," as the Sacred Scripture says, "We live and move and have our being." Truly, as the great Dionysius the Areopagite says, "the being of all things is their superessential divinity."

XI

The light of human beings

"And the life was the light of human beings." The Son of God, whom previously you called the Word, O blessed theologian, you now call life and light. And not without reason have you changed the names, but rather in order to allow us to understand different meanings. If, indeed, you have named the Son of God "the Word," it is because the Father spoke all things through the Word. As it is written, "He spake and it was done." And now you call him "light" and "life," because this same Son, who is the Word, is the life and light of all things that are made through him. And what does he light? Not other than himself and his Father. The light, therefore is, and illuminates, itself. The light of the Word reveals itself to the world; it manifests itself to the ignorant.

When humanity abandoned God, the light of divine knowledge receded from the world. Since then, the eternal light reveals itself in a twofold manner through Scripture and through creature. Divine knowledge may be renewed in us in no other way, but through the letters of Scripture and the species of creature. Learn, therefore, to understand these divine modes of expression and to conceive of their meanings in your soul, for therein you will know the Word.

Observe the forms and beauties of sensible things, and comprehend the Word of God in them. If you do so, the truth will reveal to you in all such things only he who made them, outside of whom you have nothing to contemplate, for he himself is all things. For whatever truly is, in all things which are, is he. Indeed, just as no substantial good exists outside of him, so no essence or substance exists that is not he.

And the life was the light of human beings. Why does the

theologian add "the light of human beings," as if the light which
is the light of angels, the light of the created universe, the light
indeed of all visible and invisible existence, should be especially
and peculiarly the light of humanity. Is not the Word that gives
life to all things perhaps said especially and peculiarly to be the
light of humanity, because in human beings he declared himself
not only to them, but also to the angels and to all creatures able
to participate in divine knowledge?

For God did not appear as an angel to the angels, nor as an
angel to humanity, but as a human being to both human beings
and angels. God appeared not simply in appearance but in true
humanity, which he took upon himself completely, in unity of
substance. Thus he presented himself — cognition of himself
— to all who might know him. The light of humanity, therefore,
is our Lord Christ Jesus, who in his human nature showed
himself to all rational and intellectual creatures, revealing the
hidden mysteries of his divinity, by which he is equal to the
Father.

XII

And the light shone in darkness

"And the light shone in darkness." Listen to the Apostle: "For ye were sometimes darkness, but now ye are light in the Lord." Hear Isaiah: "Those that dwell in the land of the shadow of death, upon them hath the light shined."

The light shines in darkness. All humanity, by virtue of original sin, was in darkness — not darkness of the outer eyes which sense the forms and colors of sensible things, but darkness of the inner eyes which discern the kinds and beauties of intelligible things; not in the darkness of a gloomy atmosphere, but in the darkness of the ignorance of the truth; not in the absence of the light that reveals the corporeal world, but in the absence of the light that illumines the incorporeal world. Born of a virgin, this light shines in darkness — that is to say, in the hearts of those who know it.

And following this, since it is true that humanity is now, as it were, divided into two parts — into those whose hearts are illumined by the knowledge of the truth and those who still remain in the darkness of unholiness and faithlessness — the Evangelist adds: "And the darkness comprehended it not."

This is as if he had said: The light shines in the darkness of faithful souls, and shines there more and more, beginning in faith and leading to knowledge; but the hearts of the unholy, through faithlessness and ignorance, have not grasped the Light of the Word glorifying the flesh. "Their foolish hearts were darkened," as the Apostle says. "Professing themselves to be wise, they became fools." Such, at least, is the moral sense of darkness.

XIII

The natural contemplation of these words

But the natural contemplation of these words yields another meaning to the phrase "And the light shone in the darkness."

For human nature, even if it had not sinned, would have been unable to shine by its own strength; for human nature is not naturally light, but only participates in the light. Although human nature is capable of wisdom, it is not itself wisdom: only participation in wisdom allows it to be wise. Just as the air does not shine by itself — and is for this reason named darkness — and yet is nevertheless able to receive the light of the sun, so too our nature, considered in itself, is a substance of darkness, but is able to receive the light of wisdom. And just as the air, while it participates in the sun's rays, is not said to shine by itself — but the splendor of the sun is said to appear in it, so that it does not lose its natural obscurity but only receives the supervening light into itself — so the rational part of our nature, while possessing the presence of the Word of God, knows — not through itself but through the engrafting on it of the divine Light — intelligible things and even God himself. The Word himself says: "It is not you who speak, but the spirit of your father which speaketh in you."

By means of this one sentence the Word wishes to teach us to understand this universal truth and to have this meaning always and ineffably sounding in the ears of our hearts: It is not you who shine, but the spirit of your Father shines in you. In other words, it is he, the Father, who manifests me, the Word, to shine in you, for I am the light of the intelligible world, that is, of rational and intellectual nature. You, who know me, are not. It is I myself, through my spirit, who know myself in you — for you are not a substantial light, but only participate in the self-subsisting light.

Thus the light shines in the darkness, for the Word of God — the life and light of human beings — does not cease to shine in our nature which, investigated and considered in itself, is found to be without form and dark. Nor, despite its fall, does the Word wish to forsake human nature; nor will he ever forsake it. For he forms it, since he contains it by nature; and he reforms it by deifying grace. And since he himself is the light incomprehensible to all creatures, the darkness comprehended it not.

For God surpasses all meaning and intelligence, and alone possesses immortality. Whose light is called darkness by virtue of its excellence, since no creature can comprehend either what or how it is.

XIV

There was a man sent from God

"There was a man sent from God whose name was John."

Behold the eagle, relaxing his wings of sublimest contemplation, descend in gentle flight from the highest peaks of the mountain of theology into the deepest valley of history, from the heaven of the spiritual world to the earth.

For Divine Scripture is a certain intelligible world, constituted of its four parts, its four elements. Whose earth, as it were, in the midst, at the lowest point, like a center, is history. Surrounding it, like the waters, is the abyss of moral understanding, which the Greeks are wont to call *ethike*. And in this intelligible word, around these two, as it were, lower parts, which I have called history and ethics, floats what I call natural knowledge or knowledge of nature, which the Greeks called *physike*. Rolled around, outside and beyond all, is the celestial and burning fire of the empyrean heaven, that sublime contemplation which the Greeks named "theology," beyond which no intelligence passes.

Thus the great theologian — I mean John — in the beginning of his Gospel, touches the highest peaks of theology, and penetrates the secret spiritual heaven of heavens, ascending beyond all history, ethics, and physics. From thence, turning downward in his flight, he narrates the historical sequences just preceding the incarnation of the Word, and says: "There was a man sent from God."

XV

John introduces John

John introduces John into his theology. "Deep calleth unto deep" in the voice of the divine mysteries. John, the Evangelist, narrates the history of John, the forerunner. The one, to whom it is given to know the Word in the beginning, commemorates the one to whom it is given to come before the incarnated Word.

"There was," he says, not simply "sent from God," but "there was a man." By this the Evangelist distinguishes the one who was only a human being and came before from the other who united God and humanity in compact union and came after.

In this way the Evangelist separates the transient voice from the always and unchangingly abiding Word. He makes known that one is the morning star, appearing at the dawn of the kingdom of heaven, and declares the other to be the supervening sun of justice.

Thereby he distinguishes the witness from the one to whom he bears witness, the message from the one who sends it, the light of the lamp in the night from the brightest light that fills the worlds and destroys the darkness of death and the sin of the whole human race.

Therefore the forerunner of our Lord was a human being, not God, while the Lord, whose forerunner he was, is at once a human being and God. The forerunner was a man called by grace to pass beyond humanity into God, while he before whom he came was God by nature and was called to become human by humility and the will to our salvation and redemption.

"There was a man sent." By whom? By God. By God the Word, before whom he, the human being, came. His mission was to be the precursor. Crying aloud, he sends his voice, "the voice of one crying in the wilderness," before. The messenger prepared the coming of his Lord.

"Whose name was John" — "to whom it was given" to be the forerunner of the King of Kings, to make manifest the incarnate Word. To whom it was given to baptize him as a prophetic promise of his spiritual adoption to come; and to bear witness to the eternal light by his voice and martyrdom.

XVI

The witness

"The same came for a witness, to bear witness of the Light" — that is to say, of Christ. Hear his witness: "Behold the Lamb of God which taketh away the sin of the world." And again: "He it is who coming after me was made before me." The Greek here is clearer: *emproston mou* — that is, "He was made before my sight, before my eyes."

This is as if he had openly said: "He who in the order of times was born in the flesh after my birth, him I saw before my eyes in a prophetic vision while I was still in my mother's barren innards, him I saw conceived in my sight and made a human being in the Virgin's womb."

"He was not that Light, but was sent to bear witness of that Light." This must be read and understood with the following emphasis: "He was not that Light, but *was sent* to bear witness of that Light." The forerunner of the light was not the light. Why is he then called "a burning and a shining light" and "the morning star?" He was a burning light, but he did not burn with his own light. He was the morning star, but he did not receive his light from himself. The grace of him, before whom he came, burned and shone through him. He was not the light, but a participant in the light. What gleamed in and through him was not his. As we have said before: no creature, either rational or intellectual, is in itself substantially light, but participates in the one true substantial Light which shines intelligibly everywhere and in all things.

This is why the Evangelist then adds: "That was the true Light, which lighteth every man that cometh into the world." "The true Light" is what he calls the Son of God, who subsists by himself and who, before all aeons, was born of God the Father, who also subsists by himself. "The true Light" is what he calls that same Son who, for the sake of humanity, became a human being among human beings. He is the true Light who said of himself, "I am the light of the world; he that followeth me shall not walk in darkness, but shall have the light of life."

XVII

The true Light

"That was the true Light, which lighteth every man that cometh into the world."

What does "cometh into the world" mean? What are we to understand by "every man that cometh into the world"?

Whence do human beings come into this world? Into what world do they come?

And if those are meant who come into this world from the hidden folds of nature through generation in times and places, then what sort of illumination is possible for them in this life where we are born but to die, grow but to decay, coagulate but to be dissolved again, falling from the restfulness of silent nature into the restlessness of bustling misery? Tell me, please, what kind of spiritual and true light there is for those procreated in a transitory and false life? Is not precisely this world a fit dwelling for those alienated from the true light? Is it not justly called the region of the shadow of death, the valley of tears, the abyss of ignorance, the earthly habitation that weighs down the human soul and expels the true beholding of the light from the inner eyes?

The phrase "which lighteth every man that cometh into the world" cannot therefore refer to those who proceed from hidden seminal causes into corporeal species. Rather it must refer to those who, by the spiritual regeneration through grace which is given in baptism, enter the invisible world. Rejecting the birth according to the corruptible body, these chose the second birth, which is spiritual. They tread underfoot the world which is below and ascend to the world which is above. Leaving behind the shadows of ignorance and death, they yearn for the light of wisdom and life. Ceasing to be children of human beings and beginning to be children of God, they leave behind them the world of vices, destroying these in themselves, holding before their mental eyes the world of virtues, longing with all their strength to ascend there. Thus the true light illumines those who enter this world of virtue, not those who flee into the world of vices.

XVIII

He was in the world

"He was in the world." Here the Evengelist calls "the world" not only sensible creation in general but also, and more especially, the rational nature that is in human beings. In all human beings, indeed to put it simply, in the created universe as a whole, the Word is the true light that subsists now and always has, because it never ceases to subsist in all things.

For, just as in the case of one who speaks, when he stops speaking, his voice ceases and disappears, so also with the heavenly father, should he stop speaking his Word, the effect of his Word — the created universe — would cease to subsist. For the continuous maintenance by substitution — the very continuance — of the created universe is the speech of God the Father, the eternal and unchangeable generation of his Word.

Therefore not irrationally one may proclaim the following sentence of the sensible world alone: "He was in the world and the world was made by him."

In other words: Lest anyone, partaking of the Manichean heresy, think that the world, falling into bodily perception, was created by the devil and not by the Creator of all visible and invisible things, the theologian adds: "He was in the world" — that is, he subsists in this world which contains all things — "and the world was made by him." For the Creator did not dwell in a universe made by another but in that which he himself had made.

XIX

Three worlds

Notice that the blessed Evangelist names "the world" four times. Nevertheless, we must understand that there are three worlds.

The first of these worlds in order is filled uniquely with the invisible and spiritual substances of the angelic hierarchies. Whoever enters into it possesses full participation in the true Light.

The second is directly counter to the first, for it is constituted wholly of visible and bodily natures. And yet, however low a position in the universe this world might possess, the Word was nevertheless in it, and it was made by the Word. Thus it is the first stage for those wishing to ascend to the cognition of the truth by sensible means, for the species of visible things draws the thinking soul toward the cognition of things invisible.

The third world is that which, like a mediating principle, unites in itself the upper, spiritual world and the lower, bodily world, making of these two one. By this world, humanity alone is meant, in whom all creatures are joined as one. For the human being consists of a body and a soul. Binding together the body of this world and the soul of the other world, the human being — humanity — creates a single cosmos. For the body possesses all bodily nature and the soul all spiritual nature, and these fitting together into a single harmony make up the cosmic world of the human being. That is why "man" is called "all" — for all creatures are in humanity as if melted down in a crucible. Therefore the Lord himself teaches his disciples, as they are about to go forth and preach: "Preach the Gospel to every creature."

This world, therefore, which is humanity, did not know its Creator. Neither by the symbols of the written law nor by the paradigms of visible creation did human beings, held down by the bonds of fleshly thinking, wish to know their God. "And the world knew him not."

Human beings knew God the Word neither through the nakedness of his true divinity, before he assumed human nature, nor through the garment of the incarnation, after he assumed human nature. They did not know the invisible; they denied the visible. They did not wish to seek him who sought them. They did not wish to hear him who called them. They did not wish to care for him who deified them. They did not wish to receive him who received them.

XX

His own

"He came unto his own" — unto those things, that is to say, which were made by him and so are not unworthily his own —"and his own received him not."

"His own" is humanity, whom he wished to redeem and whom he redeemed.

"But as many as received him, to them gave he power to become the sons of God, even to them that believe on his name."

Here a division is made, not in the humanity of the rational world, but in its will. Those who receive the incarnate Word are separated from those who reject it. The faithful believe that the Word has come and freely receive their Lord. The ungodly deny and stubbornly refuse him — the Jews through envy, the Pagan through ignorance. To those who received him, he gave the power to become sons of God. To those who did not receive him, he gave the opportunity to receive him one day.

For the possibility of believing in the Son of God and of becoming a son of God is denied to no one — for this is made of the human will, together with the cooperation of divine Grace.

To whom, then, is given the power to become sons of God? To those who receive him and believe in his name. Many receive the Christ. The Arians, for instance, receive him, but they do not believe in his name. They do not believe that he is the only begotten Son of God, consubstantial with the Father. They deny his *homoousion* — his co-essentiality with the Father — and affirm his *heteroousion* — his being of another essence than the Father. By this token it profits them not to receive the Christ, for they strive to deny his name. Those who truly receive the Christ — true God and true human being — and believe this most firmly: to these is given the possibility of becoming sons of God.

XXI

The Word made flesh

"Which were born, not of blood, nor of the will of the flesh, nor of the will of man, but of God."

In the ancient Greek manuscripts it says simply: "Which were born, not of blood, but of God."

"Not of blood," says the Evangelist, not by bodily procreation are those born who by merit of their faith gained adoption as the sons of God. They are born of God the Father, through the Holy Spirit, as co-inheritors with Christ: in co-filiation with the only-begotten Son of God.

"Nor of the will of the flesh, nor of the will of man." Here the Evangelist introduces two sexes from which the many born carnally are born in the flesh. For by the word "flesh" the Evangelist means the female condition, and by the word "man" the male condition.

And in case you are tempted to say that it is impossible that mortals should become immortals, that corruptible beings should become free of corruption, that simple human beings should become sons of God, and that temporal creatures should possess eternity — whichever of these doubts poses the greatest temptation for you — accept the argument which faith prepares for what you doubt: "And the Word was made flesh."

If what is greatest has undoubtedly already gone before, why should it seem incredible that what is less should be able to come after? If the Son of God is made a human being, which none of those who receive him doubt, why is it astonishing that a human being who believes in the Son of God should become a son of God? For this very purpose, indeed, the Word descended into the flesh: that in him the flesh — the human being — believing through the flesh in the Word, might ascend; that, through him who was the only begotten Son by nature, many might become sons by adoption.

It was not on his account that the Word was made flesh, but on our account, for it is only through the flesh of the Word that we can be transmuted into sons of God. Alone he came down; but with many he goes up. He, who from God made himself a human being, makes gods from human beings.

"And dwelt among us": that is, possessed our nature, so as to make us participants in his nature.

XXII

His glory

"And we beheld his glory, the glory of the only begotten of the Father."

Where did you see, O blessed theologian, the glory of the incarnate Word, the glory of the Son of God made a human being? With what eyes did you perceive it?

With bodily eyes, I believe, at the time of the Transfiguration on the mountain. For you were there then, the third witness to the divine glorification. And you were present also, I think, in Jerusalem when you heard the voice of the Father glorifying his Son by these words: "I have glorified him and I shall glorify him again." You heard the crowds of children crying: "Hosanna to the son of David."

And what may I say of the glory of the Resurrection? You saw him rising from the dead when, locked in as you were with the other disciples, he entered in to you through closed doors. You saw his glory as he ascended to the Father when he was taken up by angels into heaven. But above all these you saw his glory when, by the highest vision of the mind, you contemplated him — I mean, the Word — in his beginning, with his Father. There you saw the glory that he has "as the only begotten of the Father."

XXIII

Full of grace and truth

"Full of grace and truth." The meaning of this phrase is twofold. For it may be understood of the humanity and divinity of the incarnate Word — in which case the fullness of grace refers to his humanity and the fullness of truth to his divinity. For the incarnate Word, our Lord Jesus Christ, received the fullness of grace according to his humanity, since he is the head of the church and the firstborn of universal creation — that is, of the totality of universal humanity, which is in him and through him healed and restored.

I say "in him" because he is the greatest and principal example of the grace by which, without any preceding merits, a human being becomes God. In him this is manifested primordially.

"Through him," I say, because of his fullness we have all received the grace of deification in exchange for the grace of faith, by which we believe in him, and the grace of action, by which we keep his commandments.

The fullness of the grace of Christ, however, may also be understood to refer to the Holy Spirit. For the Holy Spirit, since it distributes and operates the gifts of grace, is often called grace. This Spirit, by its sevenfold operation, filled the humanity of Christ and rested in him. As the prophet says: "And the spirit of the Lord shall rest upon him, the spirit of wisdom and understanding, the spirit of counsel and might, the spirit of knowledge and of the fear of the Lord."

If, therefore, you wish to understand Christ himself by the phrase "full of grace," know that it refers to the fullness of his deification and of his sanctification as a human being.

Of his deification, I say that humanity and God were joined in the unity of a single substance. Of his sanctification, that not only was he conceived by the Holy Spirit but that in truth he was filled with the fullness of its gifts and that, as if at the summit of the mystical candle of the church, the lamps of grace shine in and from him.

If, however, you wish to understand the fullness of the grace and truth of the incarnate Word as referring to the New Testament, as the Evangelist himself seems to have thought a little later when he says, "For the law was given by Moses, but truth and grace came by Christ," then it would not be inappropriate to say that the fullness of the grace of the New Testament was given through Christ and that the truth of the symbols of the law were fulfilled in him. For as the Apostle says, "In him dwelleth the fullness of the Godhead bodily."

Here the Apostle calls the fullness of the Godhead the revelation hidden in the shadows. Christ, coming and dwelling in the flesh, reveals this Godhead bodily, teaching and manifesting that he in himself is the revelation. For he himself is the fountain and fullness of grace, the truth of the symbols of the law, the end of prophetic vision. To him be glory, with the Father and the Holy Spirit, for now and evermore. Amen.

Reflections

PART ONE: THE WAY
(*Homily*: Chapters I–V)

1

It is the darkest night of the year, the dead of winter. Earth has
breathed in her soul. Cut off from the sun's light, she lies silent
and closed. Now human beings, left to their own resources, are
at their lowest ebb. Tempted by matter, deprived of the gods,
they yearn for warmth and consolation. Then — suddenly
— the new world of Christmas Morning breaks forth and the
Sun of Righteousness rises, sounding in the ears of the universe,
in the hearing of the church, once and for always. The days
grow longer, light returns, the air grows warm with love. The
heavenly hosts, the first to know, say to themselves (in the
words of Origen), "If he has put on mortal flesh, how can we
remain doing nothing? Come, angels, let us descend from
heaven." And so they come down to the shepherds, the angels of
nations, and, praising God, announce the coming of Christ, the
true Shepherd. On earth, too, in the stable, all creation rejoices
in the moment of redemption, the turn so long awaited and so
ardently desired. Such is the divine cosmic event which Eriugena
celebrates in his *Homily* in the belief that everyone else does
also. Indeed, if the Incarnation is not for everyone and everything, it is for no one and nothing.

"Behold the might of the New Song!" cries Clement of
Alexandria, "It has made human beings out of stones, human
beings out of beasts. Those, moreover, that were as dead, not
being partakers of the true life, have come to life again, simply
by listening to this Song." Such for Clement is the ineffable
virtue of the Incarnation: it is the universal medicine and elixir
of life. By it, matter and spirit are made one. For all things first

sounded into form in the Word; and now the Word, that melodious, holy instrument of God, made flesh in time, sounds out again, recalling all things to their wholeness and their home-ground.

Truly, in the history of the universe regarded as the meaningful speech of human beings and gods, the incarnation of God's Word marks the turning-point. Speech having become flesh, flesh can become speech. Full, living meaning is restored. What God spoke outside time — in eternity — is now spoken, lives, and may be heard in time. No wonder then that human beings who felt so destitute can suddenly feel joy and certitude. Clement's emotion is not hard to understand. The savior of creation, the creator, has come. The king of the world, the teacher of humanity, the Word of God, has given himself. The cause of being has become the cause of well-being. Why? So that the supernatural, having become natural, can become supernatural once more and God, according to his desire, never deviated from, can become all in all. This is the meaning of resurrection, the meaning of meaning. What a task for human beings! What a prospect! God has spoken and it is for humanity to listen and respond, to hear his word and return his speech.

Realizing this, Rosenstock-Huessy wrote, "A Christian is a person to whom Christ speaks. The body of Christ are those who listen to Him." But more than that: through us, through cognition and consciousness, everyone and everything can and must listen, for all of creation groaned and travailed in pain for this, and all speech like all love is a single unity. Therefore Rosenstock-Huessy continues: "As speakers as well as lovers, we need assurance that we move in a continuum, that our discovery of real life and our words make sense for ever and ever. Otherwise we go mad and all spirit leaves us. It is impossible to assume that when we speak we do something different from the peoples of all times. Our speech would be up in the air, a meaningless stammering, unless we have the right to believe that all speech is legitimate and authorized as one and the same life process from the first day on which man has spoken to the last."

It is this tradition of those who listen before they speak that we must try to recover and make our own. The Word was spoken in the beginning and made all things; then was made flesh and dwelt among us. St. John beheld his glory, heard, and saw, and touched him. He wrote down some of what he saw and learnt. Then, some eight centuries later, John Scotus Eriugena, a holy Celtic sage, theologian, and philosopher — a Christian gnostic, Neoplatonist, and heir to untold written and unwritten teachings — meditated and transmitted the essence (as he could grasp it) of what St. John had taught. Now it is our turn, at this turn of the ages, when Christendom is finished and Christian teaching practically forgotten, and the wisdom of the past, Eastern and Western, echoes about, to connect with this tradition and set down for our time and way whatever we can find to know and tell. There are other traditions — monastic, liturgical, mystical, social — each of which has its authentic place as a legitimate consequence of the Word's incarnation, but Eriugena's gnostic and Platonic path — his Word-centered cosmological path of cognition — cries out above all these to be heard today. For without an understanding of the Word in consciousness, the Word in the cosmos, all other traditions fall short of their full meaning. Natural theology — the theology of nature — and theological anthropology — the theology of human beings — are not in fashion; and yet, without these, without a holistic understanding of humanity and nature's place in God, all the rest are without ground and it is pointless, and even dangerous, to speak of "social" or "ecological" Gospels.

To recover this unheard tradition is a task of intuition, interpretation, and meditation; of understanding and transformation. We shall not seek to project ourselves but, laying ourselves down, attempt to reflect the worlds of faith that St. John and Celtic Eriugena open up to us. We shall approach the field of Christianity through these two human gates, patiently waiting until entrance is granted. Thereby we shall hope to know ourselves anew, in a new way, and be reborn. All understanding is self-understanding — understanding how we understand — but if we wish to understand newly — if the New Testament is to remain truly new and a true testament — we must forget ourselves, our present understanding, and give ourselves up to meanings and ways of knowing we are ignorant of and alienated from. We must make them so much our own that we are remade by them. Then our knowing will cease to be merely information and will instead become a way of being. These reflections, then, constitute not a commentary but a search for life. The Word calls us because we seek the Word that is able to call us. Meeting this Word, we meet the living God, and interpretation becomes encounter.

None of this means much today because we have lost Christianity. Yet it is the thesis of Eriugena's *Homily*, which we must lay down to begin with, that it is only in and through the Word, the primordial singing principle of relation and expression — meaning — that the true religion is to be found that binds together in a single, indivisible yet distinguishable unity Father, Son, Holy Spirit, and Humanity-the-Universe. Certainly, it is not easy to find this Logos-Spirit and ourselves again. There is much that we have forgotten and more that we have yet to learn. And so we shall have to start from the beginning, and the way will often appear obscure and alien, but — trusting in what we seek — we may strive patiently in the certainty of finding the one who opens and makes wise all who open to him.

It is this omnipresent, spiritual principle of finding and knowing — the spiritual Eagle — that we have forgotten today. This is why his voice must always strike in the hearing of the church — the consciousness of the universe as mediated by human beings. He is always with us — even to the end of the world — continuously begotten in an everlasting begetting as brightness is begotten of light. As the life and truth of all things, he warms and lights his creation through a continuous act of love. To know this is to come to inhabit the limitless field of creativity outside time and nature but ever forming and creating it. It is to die to oneself and to find one's true other, one's true place and origin in the cause, essence, and source of all. It is to meet the bridegroom secretly: to dwell in paradise by the tree of life planted in every soul.

2

The mystery, the absurd premise of this proclamation, is that universal creation turns upon certain apparently very human, material, and even shabby, but in fact most divine, events, occurring for a brief moment in an obscure corner of the Middle East. This is the true apocalypse or revelation: that for this simple world-creating deed, as preparation or by default, millions of years and untold metamorphoses of evolution were required. Millions of years — so much pain, hope and suffering, so many evolutionary leaps and bounds — seem likewise to lie ahead. Perhaps we misunderstand the nature of time. Perhaps. But what is important is that only humanity stands between, unites and gives meaning to these two unthinkable extents.

3

Before one may answer, one must be called. But what does it mean to be called? It means to listen, to hear the sound of one's name uttered, and to respond to that call. In the case of the spiritual Eagle, whose voice sounds in the hearing of the church, the shaping sound, the name called, is that of the Word, who is the mouth and name of the Father, the Origin of all. What strikes in the ears of the church, changing it utterly, is none other than the first name of all as St. John speaks it at the beginning of his Gospel. One may listen in different ways and at different levels and the phrase "spiritual eagle" describes such a way and level, one appropriate to the Word of God and therefore capable of union and community with it. In the Middle Ages, indeed, Christ himself was called the Eagle. Rightly so, for it is he whom St. John proclaims. But only like may proclaim like — only like may receive like — and so the eagle both proclaims and is proclaimed, both gives and receives. The eagle in St. John proclaims the divine Eagle, Christ, the eagle of creation, to the eagle in us, in the hope that we may learn to say with St. Paul, "Not I, but the Christ in me."

4

Of John the Baptist, the voice crying in the wilderness, Eriugena writes in his *Commentary*:

> He left behind him all the realities which are contained within the limits of the world and was raised up to the heights. He became the voice of the Word, no longer recognizing in himself any substance other than that which he received by an abundant grace from beyond all creatures.

Emptied of himself in the desert wilderness of highest contemplation, John the Baptist was filled with the Word, the intellect or meaning of all things. He became its vehicle or voice, its interpreter. As Eriugena explains, "The voice is the interpreter of the spirit. All that spirit has first thought and ordered invisibly within itself, it offers by means of the voice to the senses of its hearers."

St. John the Evangelist, too, heard the voice of the Word. Responding to its call, he appropriated and entered into it. Fully listening and divested of all that was not the Word, he became one with the divine-spiritual field of its nature. Thus, in the state of pure reciprocity which contains the meaning-being of all things, St. John became the ear of the Word. Becoming its ear, he spoke; and, speaking, he became its mouth and voice: the voice of the Eagle.

5

In this way and without warning we are plunged into the central mystery of Christianity: the meeting of the human soul with Christ in the phenomenal world. How does this take place? Consider Eriugena's interpretation of the story of Christ and the woman of Samaria at Jacob's well. It is the sixth hour, the cosmic midday, the sixth or present age. Christ, tired by the rigors of incarnation, meets the woman — the human soul — by the well of the world. Seated upon its rim, he asks her for water. Surprised, she wonders why he, a Jew, would ask water of her, a Samaritan. He replies that if she knew whom he really was, she would ask him in turn for "living" water. The woman then notices that Jesus has no way of drawing any kind of water. But he repeats that the water he offers is living: a well continuously springing up into eternal life. Finally, the woman asks him for some, and he replies, "Go, call thy husband." That is, he says to her that she cannot drink his water unless she first calls her husband. If she wishes to drink, she must call her husband and return with him; then both can drink fully.

Eriugena explains this as follows:

> The woman is the rational soul [*anima*], whose husband [literally, *vir* or "man" (with the connotation of "active power") not *maritus* or *conjunx*] is understood to be the *animus*, which is variously named now intellect [*intellectus*], now mind [*mens*], now *animus* and often even spirit [*spiritus*]. This is the husband of whom the Apostle says, "The head of the woman is the man, the head of the man is Christ, the head of Christ is God." In other words, the head of the *anima* is the *intellectus*, and the head of the

intellectus is Christ. Such is the natural order of the human creature. The soul must be submitted to the rule of the mind, the mind to Christ, and thereby the whole being is submitted through Christ to God the Father.... Spirit revolves perpetually about God and is therefore well named the husband and guide of the other parts of the soul, since between it and its creator no creature is interposed. Reason in turn revolves around the knowledge and causes of created things, and whatever spirit receives through eternal contemplation it transmits to reason and reason commends to memory. The third part of the soul is interior sense, which is subordinate to reason as the faculty which is superior to it, and by means of reason is also subordinate to spirit. Finally, below this interior sense in the natural order is the exterior sense, through which the whole soul nourishes and rules the fivefold bodily senses and animates the whole body. Since, therefore, reason can receive nothing of the gifts from on high unless through her husband, the spirit, which holds the chief place of all nature, the woman or *anima* is rightly ordered to call her husband or *intellectus* with whom and by whom she may drink spiritual gifts and without whom she may in no wise participate in gifts from on high. For this reason Jesus says to her, "Call your husband, come hither." Do not have the presumption to come to me without your husband. For, if the intellect is absent, one may not ascend to the heights of theology, nor participate in spiritual gifts.

A person, then, unfolded, is a threefold being of body, soul and spirit, enjoying a direct, unmediated relationship with Christ or the Word, who is God and the knowledge and wisdom of God. Examined more closely, however, the picture becomes more complex, for between exterior sense (or body) and spirit Eriugena interposes an interpenetrated hierarchy of soul-states. Nevertheless human nature is not multiple or many, because neither by its constitution nor by its history is it a thing or object. It is a potentiality, manifesting now as one state, now as another. As such, the essential unity of human nature is "a simple nature, free from all compound." Without linking parts, human nature is everywhere present to God and present in all things. As Eriugena writes:

> As a whole it is life, intellect, reason, sense and memory; as a whole it endows body with life, nourishes it, holds it together and causes it to grow; as a whole, with all the senses, it perceives the appearances of sensible things; as a whole, beyond any corporeal sense, it treats, discerns, joins and distinguishes the nature and reason of things; as a whole, outside and above all creation and itself, it revolves about its creator in an intelligible and eternal motion. . . .

Naturally simple, the soul passes through different states and is called by different names: mind, spirit, or intellect, when it contemplates divinity; reason, when it considers created things; sense when it perceives and acts in the world of the senses; life, when it endows with life. It is the first of these states that Eriugena calls the "Eagle." The Eagle is the place where the Creator makes all knowledge. Here the intellect stands face to face with God in the Word and everything which is in the Word as cause is in the intellect as effect. Its innate knowledge is total. Intellect and God, indeed, are like two sides of one coin. What is in the one is in the other — so that it is difficult to tell them apart. The difference is that in the intellect knowledge or gnosis is created whereas in God it is uncreated. As Eriugena stresses, "The intellect is not the maker but the discoverer of natural arts, but it finds them within, not outside itself." Yet there is more to the intellect than this aspect of created knowledge for, as Eriugena repeatedly states, between the intellect and the divine, nothing interposes itself: only the intellect may know the divine. This is the divine spark of which Meister Eckhart says: "There is a power in the mind which touches neither time nor flesh; it emanates from the spirit, and remains in the spirit, and is totally spiritual. In this power God is fully verdant and flowering, in all the joy and honor that he is in himself." Such is the Eagle — that highest and most spiritual, god-like state, which medieval exegesis likens to the nobleman of the parable who went into a far country to receive for himself a kingdom and to return. Meister Eckhart quotes Ezekiel's saying, "A great eagle, with great wings full of diverse colors, came to an undefiled mountain and seized the culmen of the highest tree, breaking it off and bearing it down," and comments: "What our Lord calls a nobleman, the prophet calls a great eagle. Who ranks above him? For he is born on the one side from the highest and best in the domain of creatures and on the other side from the inmost core of the divine nature in its solitude." This is our spiritual identity, the place where we are closest to reality and to God. It is that divine, yet created spirit which, as St. Paul says, is in us and "intercedes for us with ineffable groaning." St. Jerome calls it conscience, St. Augustine the spiritual intelligence.

Intelligence, conscience, identity — the Eagle is all of these. It is our true self, where we are revealed to be one with the universe, for by it we are given a direct, unmediated participation in the source of all. Thus Dionysius, Eriugena's mentor, affirms: "The form of the eagle signifies royalty and high soaring and swiftness of flight, and the eager seizing of that food which renews strength, discretion and ease of movement with the strong intensity of vision which has the power to gaze unhindered, directly and unflinchingly upon the full brilliant splendor of the Divine Sun."

Truly, then, the Eagle is a solar bird and represents the highest power or function of consciousness — that of seeing "not through a glass darkly but face to face." It is a saving perception, "an inner sight through which the mind perceives the truth which the divine light reveals to it." Therefore Isaiah proclaims, "They that wait upon the Lord renew their strength; they shall mount up with wings as eagles." And God himself declares to Moses on Mount Sinai, "I bare you up on eagles' wings and brought you to myself." For just as the Eagle, borne aloft by powerful wings, soars towards the physical sun so, when our thinking is purified and inspired, we find ourselves borne toward the bright, creative light of the spiritual sun. Indeed, we may think of this Eagle as the light of thought transformed, as its levity or antigravific nature, its wings of love.

6

Though nothing is interposed between the Eagle and the Truth, the Eagle nevertheless depends upon the soul, its spouse, for the experience of the truth. For only in the presence of the soul, in the soul herself, is truth disclosed. Indeed, we may say that the Truth, like the soul herself, *is* the presence or experience of disclosure. Stranger still, in view of this, is the fact that the soul depends for her presence, and so for truth's disclosure, upon the body which she must consecrate by her activity, or by the spirit's working in her, calling the spirit so that the Word might consecrate the whole person.

Now body, soul and spirit in the universe are one, as God and we are one. St. Paul writes to the Ephesians, "There is one body and one spirit, even as ye are called in one hope of your calling; one Lord, one faith, one baptism, one God and Father who is over all, and through all, and in you all." Persons come singly to God, before whom each stands alone, one-on-one; and to each is given "grace according to the measure of the gift of Christ ... for the edifying of the body of Christ ... unto the perfect man, unto the measure of the fullness of the stature of Christ." Collectively, as individually, human beings constitute a single organism — a whole — with a single end, which is unity. One cannot add human beings into a quantitative multiplicity. Spiritual relations are multiplicative and $1 \times 1 \times 1 \times 1 \ldots$, continued indefinitely, will never result in any number other than one. Though bodies seem to be many, body in the universe is one; there is neither my body nor your body but simply a universal human body, the body of the universe. Likewise spirit, too, is a single unity, just as each one of us is a unity. There is just one multidimensional universe, as we are each one of us just one multidimensional being.

For Christians the process, individual and collective, of becoming one and returning to God, who is one, is founded on the building up of the body of Christ, who is the head of his body and the leaven of its building up. That body, built up, St. Paul calls the church. And as the husband (*animus*) is the head of the wife (*anima*), so the Word is the head or husband of the church. The mystery of soul and spirit — *anima* and *animus* — is one with that of the Word and his church. Thus the church, in whose hearing the voice of the spiritual Eagle sounds, is the body of the Word, which is the one body, the universe, but the universe redeemed and transformed by its union — or marriage — with Word. The Word seeks for himself a glorious body or bride, a heavenly church. He seeks to transform or leaven it until it becomes a spiritual, living, resurrection body of immortal life — not the body of sin and death we know at present.

But how to conceive of such a body? St. Paul proposes a strict analogy between the union of spirit and soul and that of Christ and his church, his body. Herewith our multifold, hierarchical universe collapses into a simple polarity, the mystery of the number two. Through this the universe came into being. "Great is the mystery of marriage!" states the *Gospel of Philip*, "For without it the world would not have come into being." As Eriugena writes in the *Periphyseon*, "the first and greatest division of universal nature is into the creator of the founded universe and the nature created in that founded universe." But two without three, as Plato knew, is impossible. Spirit and body, uncreated and created, cannot exist without a third coming into existence. Spirit, soul, and body — these three are simultaneous and inseparable natures. But with the fall, they fell apart. The universe became dualized, sexualized. "Matter" arose and the resurrection of the body or "flesh" was an absurdity. But with the Incarnation, the turn was taken: the Word was made flesh.

Body or "flesh" is not the "meat" of which we are made, but who we are, our outer, "made" wholeness. Flesh is thus our existence considered in its contrast to God, in its difference and distance, and so in its relation. With the incarnation of the Uncreated, the beautiful created bride — the body-soul, the created "flesh" — is suddenly interpenetrated with a Christic ferment. Spirit has descended into flesh, incarnated, so that flesh, quickened and obedient, might ascend to spirit — a process which is realized, as both St. Paul and Eriugena teach, first in faith and then in knowledge, for faith is the soul's mode of listening or obedience, while knowledge is the spirit's. Each soul, moreover, has her own spirit (or husband), whose flesh she is; and each spirit must leave the kingdom of the divine to seek his soul-sister-bride, and become one flesh or body — the body of the Word — with her.

Thus the voice of the Word strikes in the hearing of the church of human nature, the cosmos, to call her to a sacred marriage. But such is the nature of this mysterious hierogamy that for the Word to call her, she must call him. The two must become one again, one voice. Eve must reunite with Adam, Sophia with Christ. "When Eve was still in Adam, death did not exist. When she was separated from him, death came into being. If he again becomes complete and attains his former self, death will be no more." So states the *Gospel of Philip*, giving evidence of a period of Christian life when such knowledge was not forgotten. This is the call of the Eagle.

7

Specifically, it is in the "hearing" of the church that the voice strikes. This is the *auditum*, the French *ouie*, the SENSE of hearing, the fifth sense, which corresponds to the quintessence. For as touch is to earth, taste to water, smell to air, sight to fire, so "hearing belongs to the fifth element, the Word become physically, tactilely sensible through sound." Schwaller de Lubicz adds: "The four senses pass by the brain; but the fifth sense, hearing, passes by the 'heart' without speaking directly to the brain. This is the spiritual sense, which is the gateway to the intelligence of the Heart."

Hearing, then, is the way to the *intellectus*, and so to the Word, the active and immaterial fire, the properly human essence. The Word, from this point of view, is the quintessence which interpenetrates the other elements, constituting the meaning of things. "You wish to see? — Listen!" advised St. Bernard.

8

The sound of the Eagle's voice is a transient, momentary phenomenon, which our outer senses by their structure are enabled to grasp. But this transient vibration, which strikes our hearing, is the temporal embodiment of a timeless pattern. It is a sign to be read, a message to be interpreted. From this it follows that the sound and, by implication, the whole phenomenal realm, is potentially (if appropriately interpreted) a theophany or hierophany, a text or language manifesting and revealing something divine or sacred. As such, phenomena are symbols, binding temporal and timeless realms together; and what needs to be understood is understanding itself, the apprehension of the meaning at once hidden and disclosed in the interwoven pattern; for the sign or symbol lies not in the sound but in the knowledge — the process of understanding — which, by means of spirit, soul, and sense, a person is able to realize through it. The sound, indeed, conceals as much as it reveals, for it is precisely not what it announces. It is an appearance, veiling and unveiling what it brings to the senses. The task of understanding, then, is to reveal what is concealed, an act of interpretation which is essentially alchemical. For alchemy is the art of occulting the apparent while revealing the hidden. Put another way, what is involved is the process of extracting "light" from "matter," in which it is buried. Thus, not surprisingly, "to make the eagle fly" in alchemy means "to extract light from the tomb and bring it to the surface." More significantly, perhaps, such a union is termed a "spiritual light" — in conformity with which the alchemist Fulcanelli derives the word "eagle" from the Greek *aigle*, meaning "brightness, clarity, a torch."

9

Now, it is the *animus* — the action of the intellect or spirit — and not the rational soul or *anima* which penetrates by intuition the timeless meaning made available through the senses. Or rather, it is only by means of the action of *animus* that the *anima* is able to grasp the timeless meaning given in the symbols of the senses. The *animus* discloses — reveals — what to the *anima* is concealed. Indeed, in a sense, the *animus* is that disclosure or revelation, but not the *animus* alone, for it has a "head" and that head is the Word. As Eriugena notes in the *Periphyseon*, though it is the seeker's duty to investigate, "the finding belongs only to him 'who lightens what is hidden in the shadows.'" The Word, the light shining in the darkness, "alone can open sense and intellect." Meaning of this kind is called *significatio passiva* — passive meaning, meaning that is given to us, that we *receive* as revelation. This is the existential meaning whereby we know what is made in us and our experience and our knowledge are one. By this knowledge we are remade by what we seek to understand and are brought into identity with it. In a word, "Our truth and highest essence is given specific form by contemplation of the truth."

The Latin of the *Homily* confirms this gnostic dimension of knowing, for the word Eriugena chooses to use for "meaning" or "revelation" is *intellectus*, which also means "mind" or "spirit." Thus a single term connotes both the organ and the object of higher knowledge, which is therefore not a dualized knowing of subject and object, but a union or identity. As Eriugena says: "Whenever pure intellect knows something perfectly, it is made in that thing and becomes one with it." This is the principle by which one becomes what one beholds — which is a mixed blessing, for one may equally behold parts of one's lower nature as of one's higher nature. Nevertheless, where the lowest is possible the highest is also. At its highest, specifically in contemplation of the truth, such knowing is *theosis* or deification. In the words of the *Gospel of Philip*: "It is not actually possible for anyone to see any of the things that actually exist unless he becomes like them. This is not the way with human beings in this world: they see the sun without becoming the sun; they see the heaven, and earth, and all other things, but they are not these things. You saw the spirit, you became the spirit. You saw Christ, you became Christ."

The relation to Christ is primary: as the Word is the image of the Father, humanity is the image of the Word. As all things are made and known in and through the Word, so are they made and known in and through human beings. This is the view of Eriugena: "As the creative wisdom, God's Word saw all things that were made in it before they were made, and the vision itself of the things seen before they were made is their true, changeless and immortal essence, so created wisdom, which is human nature, knew all things in it before they were made." Thus as Christ's knowledge is creation, so human knowing in the Word is a second creation, and *gnosis* or intellection is at once a remembering and a creating anew.

The mystery for us lies in the paradoxical manner in which, as creatures, we split the seamless web of reality into two along the lines of our perceiving. It is this that gives rise in such a confusing way to two realms, the one (as Plato put it) always becoming and never real, the other always real and never becoming. Yet even for Plato these two, though distinct at some level of human cognitive organization, are nevertheless indivisible and wholly interpenetrated. The one is cause, the other effect; but cause contains effect, and effect leads back to cause. This is the reason, in St. Paul's words, why "the invisible things of him from the creation of the world are clearly seen, being understood from the things which are made."

How to understand this? Eriugena writes: "Everything which is either participates or is participated in, or is participation, or simultaneously is participated in and participates." Participation, then, is an essential concept. Eriugena defines it as "simply the derivation from the higher essence to the essence following after it, and the distribution from that which first has being to that which follows." In other words, participation is a kind of causality-emanation by which things come into existence by 'participation' in a higher essence. As Socrates says in the *Phaedo*, "There is no other way any given object can come into being except by participation in the reality particular to its appropriate universal." Such participation is what the Pythagoreans called "imitation," when they said that all things imitated numbers. It is the way in which universal and particular, enduring and transient, may be bound together in a unity while maintaining their distinction. In this way, divine and human, though distinct, are united in the Word, and body and soul, though distinct, are united in human nature.

The idea of distinction is important because it indicates that reality continuously and inevitably reflects — mirrors — itself, setting up consequential chains of participation by which it unfolds through intermediaries from the highest and only principle of all, the Word. This is the view of the *Gospel of Philip*, when it says, "Truth did not come into the world naked, but it came in types and images," for images are participations — angels — the source of whose reflected light is the Light of the World, Truth itself. There is no other. Eriugena writes: "All things come from a single First Principle, and nothing is found in the nature of things visible and invisible, by whatever kind of generation it emerges into its own species, which is not stationed eternally in the only-begotten Word of God, in whom all things are one." As participation or image, then, the world is truly the Bride of God, and not illusion. Mystical exegesis and the ascent to true meaning through encounter with image and angelic being is therefore necessary and possible; and the sense world groans and travails in pain to be transmuted by the imaginative perception of human knowing in the Word.

Such human knowing is possible because, in this round-dance — *perichoresis* — of creation, the cause, as the substance, is one, a unity, so perfect that it can only be God. Making all, God is made in all. The one who is superessential, hidden, formless, unknowable, is also knowledge, form, appearance. Proceeding into all things, this "one" makes himself in all things, while ever remaining transcendently hidden in himself.

To clarify this, Eriugena often favors an example "drawn from our own nature," as when he writes:

> Our intellect, too, though invisible and incomprehensible in itself, is both manifested and comprehended by certain signs when it is, as it were, embodied in sounds or letters or gestures. But although it thus became apparent without, it always remains invisible within; and while it bursts out in various forms comprehensible by the senses, it does not abandon the always incomprehensible condition of its nature.... Hence it is both silent and it shouts, and it shouts while it is silent; and though invisible it is seen, and while it is seen it is invisible; and though uncircumscribed it is circumscribed, and while circumscribed it remains uncircumscribed.

Through the symbol, the unmanifest is manifested while remaining unmanifest. Through the transient word the uncreated,
eternal Word is heard.

In a sense, then, the distinction between transient sound
and enduring meaning is ambiguous. As a single process, God's
purpose is timeless or, rather, is time itself. The mystery, for us,
is its appearance in passing time. This confuses us, causing us to
separate ourselves from it, to set up time and history as
independent entities, instead of realizing our identity with
them. Humanity is the evolution of the universe. It is not that
the universe in its evolution gave rise to human beings, but
rather that human beings in the process of their becoming have
manifested the universe. The universe is the revelation of God
through human nature. This is why, according to Eriugena, the
reality of God and the world is one — if only we are open and
become the place of their disclosure, the theater of their play.

To that place we must fly. Therefore human nature or,
more particularly, the soul, is always winged. Plato wrote,
"When it is perfect and winged, it journeys on high and controls
the whole world, but one that has shed its wings sinks down
until it can fasten on something solid, and settling there it takes
itself an earthly body."

10

The bird of the *Homily* soars on wings of innermost theology:
knowledge of God sustains this bird in its flight. But since God
cannot be known except as he allows himself to be known, we
must understand this sustaining knowledge to be given by God,
and not in any sense won from him. Innermost theology is
therefore the receiving of God's greatest gift, his Word.

To practice such theology is to open oneself to God's most
intimate revelation or disclosure, which is wisdom. Wisdom is
the substance of theology. It is what moves it, for as Eriugena

points out, "The name wisdom is properly given to that power by which the contemplative mind, whether of human being or angel, considers the divine, eternal, and unchangeable, whether it is concerned with the first cause of all or the primordial causes of things which the Father created in his Word at once and together." Theology is therefore not a dry, abstract science, but the crown of mysticism, the most concrete experience, proceeding as the *Homily* puts it, "by intuitions of most brilliant and highest contemplation."

Theology, wisdom, contemplation — these characterize the higher states of the soul's existence. By these the purified soul in continuous and attentive love gives birth to knowledge in mystic certitude and faith. Such faith is not, of course, blind belief, or indeed belief of any kind, but is rather the power of perfect *selflessness*: the selflessness that permits unitive vision or intuition, the eye that becomes what it beholds.

11

St. John, however, transcends all vision and goes beyond all contemplation. He goes beyond everything, including creation itself. In this state beyond vision, on the other shore, much of God or meaning may be revealed, but infinitely more always escapes knowing and meaning. God is always hidden, obscure, mysterious. Only by theophanies — divine showings forth — does he make himself known. Such is the bosom of the Father, a cloud of unknowing for the ordinary mind, but a paradise, true heaven, for an eagle of high flight.

The mystical flight of the soul, once it has started, has neither end nor destination but is a perpetual motion toward an infinite perfection. This is the doctrine of Gregory of Nyssa, for whom there are no limits to the Good, nor bounds to the itinerary, but only "a perpetual increase of goods for all the eternity of aeons": an endless coursing in the divine darkness of the Father's breast. "This is the true knowledge of what is sought," he writes, "this is the seeing that consists in not seeing, because that which is sought transcends all knowledge, being separated on all sides by incomprehensibility as by a kind of darkness." This darkness, beyond God known and qualified, into which St. John ascends, is the hidden, nameless abyss of the Godhead prior to all opposition.

God and Godhead must not here be confused for, as Meister Eckhart wrote, "they are as distinct as heaven and earth." Godhead is God as he is in himself, in the intimate solitude and hidden wilderness of his own ground. The God we can know, on the other hand, is God in his relations. Here he sees in himself all things endowed with being and "runs into all things and does not stand still, but fills all things by running." The first is a mystery, a secret, the arcanum; the second is nature. St. John passes from nature into the arcanum where, in the unspeakable ground of all, he hears "unspeakable words (*arcana verbi*)," not lawful for human beings to utter. And yet — a paradox — he utters them. Entering what can neither be distinguished nor spoken, St. John clearly distinguishes and speaks. How can this be?

Here we must digress into the doctrine of theophany. Eriugena writes in the *Periphyseon*:

> If the cause of all things is inaccessible to all things that are created by it, then there can be no doubt that the reasons of all things which exist in it eternally and without change are completely inaccessible to all things of which they are the reasons. And yet anyone who might say that in the intellects of angels there are certain *theophanies* of those reasons, that is to say, certain divine manifestations which are comprehensible to the intellectual nature, but are not the reasons themselves, will not, I think, stray from the truth.

Indeed, from Eriugena's perspective, just as for God all is God, so for created beings everything — the whole of creation, everything that is and is not — is a theophany, marvelously showing forth the divine while at the same time concealing it. The messenger both is and is not the message. Creation is not God, but it is angelic, prophetic, revelatory, and through it God speaks. In his *Commentary* Eriugena asks what it is that human beings and angels see when they think they see God (who "has never appeared in himself to anyone whatsoever and never would and never will so appear"). How then will God appear to those who are chosen? "He will appear in his *theophanies*, that is, in divine apparitions in which, according to the purity and virtue of each, he will appear. In the same way perfectly purified souls and intelligences are theophanies; in them God manifests himself to those who seek and love him; in them, as in clouds, the saints are caught up. . . ."

Theophany, like meaning, then, is a species of grace or revelation. Dionysius says, "All divine things, even those that are revealed to us, are known only by their communications. Their ultimate nature, which they possess in their own original being, is beyond mind, and beyond all being and knowledge." Therefore, he continues, "If we call the superessential mystery by the name of God, or Life, or Being, or Light, or Word, we conceive of nothing else than the powers that stream therefrom to us, bestowing Godhead, Being, Life, or Wisdom; while the mystery itself we strive to apprehend by casting aside all the activities of our minds." Two actions thus combine to form theophany: the down-streaming of "powers" and the upward-striving of the human person. As Maximus, another of Eriugena's mentors, puts it: "*Theophany* originates only from God, and is brought about by the condescension of the divine Word — the only begotten Son, the wisdom of the Father — toward the human nature created and purified by him, and by the exaltation of human nature towards the Word through divine love." And again: "Divine wisdom descends through mercy as far as the human intellect ascends through love."

Condescension, exaltation; grace descending, nature rising; God and creation: these constitute the systole and diastole of theophany, the sacramental round-dance of creation — whose end is now revealed to be *theosis* or deification. Creation striving upward in love is bathed in the fine descending mist of deificent grace. Mercy and love. As Eriugena says: "This is the cause and substance of all virtues. Every theophany, every virtue, both in this life and in the future life, is produced not outside a human being but in him or her and arises both from God and from human beings themselves."

Thus there is a theology more perfect than that called "negative theology" that strips reality of all attributes and sensible habits of thought and frees the soul and spirit, now conjoined, for knowledge of supra-intelligible reality, but cannot procure it. This only a fully "mystical theology" can do — one that, going beyond detachment and negation, is theophanic and leads to union and divinization. Such theology is prophetic: it is a gift and a possession. This is the sense in which St. John, entering the first principle of all, clearly distinguishes and interprets the first and most perfect theophany, that of the Trinity. For this reason he is called the "theologian," the amazing prophet of the Word in the beginning, the chief source of our knowledge of the Three-in-One.

12

In the beginning was the Word: in the pure, indivisible, partless unity of the Origin was the creator power of meaning or revelation (distinction). Upon this premise the Gospel of John rests. For what St. John proclaims, in the first instance, is not Jesus, the historical founder of Christianity — the teacher and profound moral example — but an immaterial, abstract, irrational, celestial principle. And yet St. John does not deny the human, historical Jesus, for a few verses later he states categorically that "the Word was made flesh and dwelt among us." Nevertheless, it is not Jesus but the Word, the LOGOS, that he announces first.

En arche en ho logos. Arche is the principle, cause, source, and origin of all: the Father. Nothing comes before it, nothing comes after. It is all. Dwelling in majestic solitude, it is absolute unity — the nothingness or *nihil per excellentiam* from which all things will be made. As such, it is the ground of all being, its primal substance, unknown, and unthinkable. And yet, in this nothingness, which is a perpetual fountain, rests an immanent power of distinction. In this nothing lies the power of something. This is the answer to the metaphysician's question, "Why is there something rather than nothing?" We may call it the power of creation, knowledge, form, order, reason, harmony, meaning, even beauty, truth, goodness: a power of expression and distinction, the *logos* or mediator, the Word.

Logos means many things. According to Plato, the word is used with four different meanings: for mental thought without words; for discourse proceeding from the mind and expressed by the voice; for the explanation of the elements of the universe; and for the ratio of proportion. Thought, discourse, meaning, relation: the *Logos* or Word is all of these and more.

Not surprisingly, then, *logos* derives from *legein*, to say aloud or utter. But *legein* also, and perhaps originally, meant "to lay down and before; to gather and bring together; to collect, to harvest, to store." This primordial utterance therefore is the storehouse or granary, the place where the Father lays down, gathers in and collects. It is the place of all places — the place where all things are placed that is itself no place. In this sense the Word or Son is the home of all things. Here all things are made: he is their resting place and place of repose, into whose breast all things return to find themselves at home. "An enchanted region where everything belonging there returns to that in which it rests," the philosopher Heidegger says, adding: "The region gathers, just as if nothing were happening, each to each and each to all into an abiding while resting in itself.... In it openness is halted and held, letting everything merge in its own resting."

This opening, gathering aspect of the Word we may call the free play or motionless movement of pure relation. It is God's creativity, his expressive activity and active expression, which will finally issue in the primal deed of the FIAT LUX: Let there be light! Within the Godhead, however, creation is held in a perfect equilibrium of absolute self-determination (freedom) which, as determination, already implies will, choice, definition and action. This is to say, it implies difference and relation: rhythm. For what distinguishes two things, revealing each to the other, separating and holding them apart, is the same as that which, mediating between them, holds them together in harmony. Only what is different may be related. As Plato writes in the *Timaeus*: "It is impossible that the determination or arrangement of two of anything, so long as there are only two, should be beautiful without a third. There must come between them, in the middle, a bond which brings them into union."

Now the holding apart, the act of distinction, judgment or comparison — that act of knowing — was also called by the Greeks *logos* or ratio. Proportion, or what binds ratios rhythmically together into unity, was therefore called *analogos* or "of like ratio," as in the *analogos* "a is to b as b is to c". Such proportion represents a more perfect relation because it embodies the principle of *logos* twice, both to separate and to unite. For this reason the most beautiful LOGOS, the only true *analogos*, was the unique proportion called the Golden Proportion, which employs only two terms, a:b:b:a + b. As Plato said, "The most beautiful bond is that which brings perfect unity to itself and the parts linked."

It is in this sense of the most beautiful bond that brings

perfect unity that the Word prays "that they may all be one; as thou, father, art in me, and I in thee, that they may be one in us . . . I in them, and thou in me, that they may be made perfect in one." This is "the lamb slain from the foundation of the world": the primordial scission of sacrifice and self-revelation made for the foundation of the world. Out of divine darkness the world worlds and becomes itself in light. God and world share this one dynamic heart and center — both rest in the activity of the Word or *Logos.*

The Word, therefore, is a verb, an action. This is why Goethe, in his *Faust*, translated "In the beginning was the word," *Im Anfang war die Tat*: In the beginning was the deed. Certainly this is true of the Hebrew *dabhar*, which comprises all Hebraic realities — word, deed and concrete object — into a single, expressive totality. Throughout the Middle East the word, and above all the Word of God, was a mighty, dynamic force. In Assyria and Babylonia it was cosmic — a storm, a rushing torrent. In Egypt, it was an ever-active, almost corporeal emanation from the Mouth of God. For the Hebrews it was more an internalized, moral force: a word of command. God spake, and it was done. Speech and deed, thought and speech, were a single creative unity. *In the beginning was the Word.*

13

Meister Eckhart writes: "I declare that it is not my present opinion that God understands because he exists, but rather that he exists because he understands. God is an intellect and understanding, and his understanding itself is the ground of his existence. St. John says, 'In the beginning was the Word and the Word was with God, and the Word was God.' He does not say, 'In the beginning was being and God was being.' A word is completely related to an intellect, where it is either the speaker or what is spoken. . . ." The conclusion is inevitable: "God, who is the creator and not creatable, is an intellect and understanding; he is not being or existence."

God knows before he is, and his knowing is the ground of his being. God's knowing, that is, is the "cause" of his being: his being is the effect (or consequence) of his knowing. Being as such, in its cause, is not being, but knowing. And the Word likewise therefore is the disclosure and revelation not of God's being but of God's knowing — a knowing beyond being that Eriugena calls "nothingness." Yet the Word is not itself knowing in our sense, for the power of disclosure or distinction is not itself distinction, it only makes these possible, containing them as potentiality. Now, the making possible of these is the creation of being, and the Word, who is the power of knowing which contains being and yet is not itself either knowing or being, is therefore always active in our knowing and being — in our making of distinctions and being made in our distinctions. God's knowing, the Word, is different from our own. In the words of Meister Eckhart: "His knowledge is the cause of things, whereas our knowledge is caused by them. Consequently, because our knowledge is dependent upon the being by which it is caused, being itself is with equal reason dependent upon God's knowledge. Hence everything in God transcends existence and is totally understanding."

Eriugena puts it differently. Knowledge precedes and is the cause of what it knows. Knowledge proceeds from an original knowing and is, if not the "remembering" of it, at least the realization of a possibility pre-existent in it. In the case of human knowing, the knowing which causes it — which is therefore in a sense original human knowledge, and from which it flowers — is none other than the direct, unmediated effect of God's knowing, the Word, whose unmediated effect is the creation of being. Human knowing, then, rests ultimately in being in the Word. But between it and the Word there is an abyss of transcendence, an abyss crossed by the incarnation of the Divine Human. God's knowing is without object or otherness. It is, we may say, pure subject. God knows, and what he knows is his knowing: a pure activity, a deed, a being. Simone Weill writes: "The verb 'to think', when God is subject, can only be taken in the active voice. What God thinks is still a being who thinks."

The Word, then, is divine consciousness, the seed of consciousness, by which we may undertand a metaphysical formative power of distinction or difference: a superessential being who thinks without otherness or object. From this power all knowing derives and receives its form — which means that no knowing is ever representation or denotation but is creation.

The Word as knowing is thus a vessel wherein the true meanings of all things are stored; or rather, more accurately, it is the infinite origin of the truth containing, as a seed contains the plant, all the meanings constitutive of it. Here there are no single ideas or isolated forms, but only simultaneity, reciprocity, identity. This is a paradoxical seed, constituted by what it contains and containing what it constitutes. Moreover, by a strange topology, this seed-place or vessel has no exterior. More peculiarly still it contains us and we contain it.

Such is this Christic vessel, the Grail of the Word.

Eriugena writes:

> Just as the intellect of all things which the Father made in his only begotten Word constitutes their essence and the foundation of everything naturally known about that essence, so that knowledge of everything that the Father's Word created in the human soul is their essence and the foundation of everything naturally discerned about it. And just as the Divine Intellect precedes everything and is everything, so the knowledge of the intellectual soul precedes everything which it knows and is everything of which it has foreknowledge. Thus everything subsists causally in Divine Intellect and in effect in human knowledge. Not, as we have often said, that the essence of all is one thing in the Word and something else in the human

being, but that the mind views one and the same essence
in one way in eternal causes and in another in their
effects. . . .

14

Above all, the Word is where I take my stand when I stand at the
center and origin of all. The Word is where I am when I am who
I am. When, giving up all, I find myself carried into the heart of
the meaning of the world, then it is by the grace of the Word
that I am sustained in its arms and at its breast outside of space
and time. For the Word is the ground and preserver of the
world. There, where all things find their home-ground, is our
home-ground too. There we have been from the beginning,
witnesses reflecting the fullness of meaning. Such is our state
from the beginning, which we have lost, from which we have
fallen and toward which we tend by our renewed Word-given
nature, any other tendency being unnatural to us and to the
world. For the world, too, is only real and meaningful to the
extent that it is known and revealed in the Word. There is no
meaning except in the Word, which is Meaning; and the
experience of meaning, lived and experienced in the deepest
way, is the experience of the Word. There is no other meaning
— if by meaning one understands the fulfillment and completion, the flowering, of the world as it rises in us. For when sheer
reality worlds it worlds in and through the Word alone. Outside
the Word there is nothing.

15

St. John, who is the Eagle, is that state of receptivity to which
something is given. Indeed, everything and more than everything is given to him. "Give us this day our daily bread," the

Lord's Prayer affirms, but we receive much more than our supersubstantial bread, or rather that bread is an inconceivably greater gift than we could ever imagine. For, truly, we are nothing but what we are given and receive. Even creation itself, which we are, receives its being "daily" from God, who creates it from nothing. Creation, like human life, is a gift, freely given: a contingent, providential thing. Such is the tradition of those who believe "A man can receive nothing unless it be given him from heaven" and St. Paul's "I know nothing by myself." Paradoxically, then, grace is the ground and substance of all: the beginning, the consummation, and the crown. For as Meister Eckhart wrote, "Outside of God there is nothing." God is all.

The key text here is that of St. James, who wrote, "Every good grant and perfect gift is from above, descending from the father of lights." All is light, then, light from light; and we are light, children of the light. That is why, as moths to a flame, we are drawn to it, like to like. To understand this, we must grasp the distinction between "grants" and "gifts," between the light which is granted us as our existence and the light which is given to us so that we may receive the light of our existence. Eriugena puts it thus: "The difference between grants and gifts is that the proper distributions by which every nature subsists are, and are called, grants; but gifts are distributions assigned by grace, by which every subsisting nature is adorned. Thus a grant is made by nature, a gift by grace, for every perfect creature is made up of nature and grace."

A grant gives nature or essence, while a gift has to do with an added power received as an empowering act of grace. Of gifts, the greatest is deification, the perfect flower of grace. Grace thus is something "extra," a superfluous gift of superabundance that may come to fulfill and complete the nature already granted. And yet, if it does fulfill that nature, it cannot be said to be truly superfluous or wholly other. There is a paradox here, the first of many. As Eriugena says, "The gift of grace is not contained within the limits of created nature, and does not operate according to natural power, but achieves its effects supernaturally, and beyond all created, natural reasons." But to do so must we not assume a similarly superessential and supernatural organ for its reception? And what else can that organ be than the very nature originally granted us as our essence — that jewel in the dungheap, buried and concealed within the toiling web of sickness, sin and death. Such is the dwelling into which thou enterest! Therefore Eriugena says: "Superessential goodness grants not only being but eternal being to all things." God, by his nature, "calls into being what previously had no being." Creating it from nothing, he grants it eternal being.

This grant of eternal being that we are — our created but eternal nature — rests upon the "Nothingness" from which God creates. This nothingness, Eriugena makes quite clear, is not some pre-existent, formless matter which is "nothing" by virtue of privation — of being without any attributes. Rather it is the absolute, infinite, unknown and unknowable transcendent excellence — the *nihil per excellentiam* — which is uncreated, and so prior to creation and privation. As Eriugena says of this unspeakable divine ground: "When it is understood as incomprehensible on account of its excellence, it is not improperly called nothing." As nothingness it is not less, but more than being. Hence it is called "superessential," "above" all the things that are and are not, prior to distinction. It is "the inaccessible brilliance of the divine Goodness," God's transcendent darkness, hidden by all light. Indeed, as uncreated God it is unknowable even to God, for as Eriugena says, as nothing, God is "in everything incomprehensible both to himself and to every intellect." From this point of view, without creation God cannot recognize himself as "something," but dwells in divine self-ignorance. And so likewise must we learn to dwell if ever we are to arrive at that grant which is our home-ground: creativity, the ability to begin. Arriving there we become fit recipients of the gifts of grace: we can begin.

Mystery of mysteries! The uncreated is created, the incommunicable communicates itself, and what is concealed by nature is disclosed by nature. The unknown God is known. How does this happen? By the divine energies (distinctions, powers) which we human beings, grounded and formed of his incommunicability, receive as gifts of uncreated grace and whose reception depends upon the soul's prior disposition to receive. As Dionysius, Eriugena's mentor, says:

> Not that the good is wholly incommunicable to anything; nay, rather, while dwelling alone by itself, and having there firmly fixed its superessential ray, it lovingly reveals itself by illuminations corresponding to *each separate creature's powers*, and thus draws upwards holy minds into such contemplation, participation, and resemblance of Itself as they can attain.

Essence to essence, energy to energy, what miracles are accomplished, what divine ends are fulfilled!

Blood has been spilled in the effort to understand that both nature and grace are given by God — and constitute the whole person. One is what we are, as paradoxical creatures created from nothing; the other is what we receive, our relationship to the one who gives and creates. Grace, which is uncreated, is what we can become, what we are destined for; nature, which is created, but out of what is uncreated, is who we are that are so destined. Therefore there is always a synergy or commingling between God-created nature and uncreated, deifying grace — between nature's effort and the freedom of grace. This dance is possible because nature — through human nature — is distinguished precisely by its freedom. God created freedom and this freedom is human nature. Grace and freedom thus presuppose each other, the freedom in the one calling the freedom in the other.

"Grace and freedom are the two wings by which the soul ascends." Or, as Eriugena puts it, the path to true understanding is "the cooperation of divine grace and the power of reason in the souls of wise believers." So it is with St. John.

16

"Mystery" derives from the Greek root *mu*, indicating a closed mouth, from which comes *muein*, meaning "to keep silent." A mystery is that of which we cannot or may not speak, about which we must keep silent for it itself is silent. And yet, silence speaks. Therefore Eriugena makes a distinction between "arcana" and "mysteries." Arcana refer to the Lord's face, his transcendence; mysteries refer to his feet, his immanence.

The phrase "hidden mysteries," which occurs in chapter two of the *Homily*, recurs in chapter eleven. There it is said of the Word that his incarnation "revealed the hidden mysteries of his divinity, by which he is equal to the Father." That is, by his incarnation the Word revealed the mystery which is in the bosom of the Father: the very mystery he is. For the Word itself is the bosom of the Father, as Eriugena affirms when he writes, "The only begotten Son is none other than the bosom of the Father, because he introduced the Father into the world. But the only begotten Son is also the bosom of the Father because he dwells forever amid the secrets of the Father's nature. As he himself says, 'I am in the Father and the Father is in me.' Indeed, just as the Son is the 'House' of the Father — for he himself says, 'In my Father's house there are many mansions' — so in the same way the Son is the bosom of the Father. In him the Father receives and gathers all those whom he wishes to receive and gather." In this way mystery, while remaining unknown, makes known the unknown. By it the transcendent is introduced into the world and becomes, while ever remaining transcendent, immanent.

The hidden mysteries of the Word, penetrated by St. John and given by him to the world, are two: his transcendence and his immanence. Namely, the Word that was in the beginning — this is 'the hidden mystery which God ordained before the world unto our glory' — and the Word made flesh and revealed thereby. As St. Paul wrote, "The mystery which hath been hid from ages and generations . . . is now made manifest."

It is to mysteries such as these that Clement refers when he says that "by initiation" they make us holy. Mystery, indeed, by definition demands initiation or decisive change. For, in order to penetrate mysteries and to be made holy by them — or to receive sacraments, perform rituals, or read symbols — one's being must change and one must become other.

We tend to forget such things, but Eriugena still remembers. Therefore he often translates *musterion* (mystery) as *sacrament.* For him the sacred is hidden, mysterious, secret: mystery is the sacred, constituting content of sacrament. Ordinary reason is powerless before it. To understand it, faith must summon the spirit in a summoning which is a laying down of itself, a waiting, that will give birth to knowledge from above: true knowledge which is true being, the highest good.

17

The good is the superessential ground of all being, the source of all gifts. There is nothing that does not derive from the good and seek the good as its end. Beyond form, the good occasions form; beyond being, life, wisdom, beauty, the good ever sees itself in these — as these. It is the Spiritual Sun, "an originating beam and an overflowing radiance," creating, animating, and perfecting all things by its divine light which fills every mind. In all things the desire for its brilliance continuously transforms darkness and ignorance — for all things by nature desire the transcendent order of the good. This is the love which moves the stars: the desire of creation to be all in all with God.

Dionysius, filled with Platonism, writes in rapture:

We dare affirm (because it is the truth) that the Creator of
the universe himself, in his beautiful and good yearning
towards the universe, is through excessive yearning of his
Goodness transported outside of himself in his providential activities towards all things that have being, and is
touched by the sweet spell of Goodness, Love, and Yearning, and so is drawn from his transcendent throne above all
things, to dwell within the heart of all things through a
substantial and ecstatic power whereby he yet stays within
himself. . . . Therefore, on the one hand, they call him the
object of Love and Yearning as being beautiful and good
and, on the other, they call him Yearning and Love as being
a motive power leading all things to himself, who is the
only ultimate beautiful and good — Yea, as being his own
self-revelation and the bounteous emanation of his own
transcendent unity, a motion of yearning, simple, self-
moved, self-acting, pre-existent in the Good, and overflowing from the Good into creation, and once again returning
to the Good. . . .

"All objects of knowledge," Plato says, "derive from the
Good not only their power of being, but their very being and
reality." As such, of course, "Goodness is not the same thing as
being, but is even beyond being, surpassing it in dignity and
power."

18

To St. Peter such high mysteries were not disclosed, for when
Peter said to Jesus, "You are the Christ, Son of the Living God,"
he was not affirming the presence before him in the flesh of the
Word in the arcanum of the one principle of all. St. Peter's
recognition of the Christ, in which he rejoiced, must for that
reason have another meaning, which Christ knew and which we
must seek in Peter himself.
  Kabbalistically the Living God is the fertilizing, active,

impregnating vitality of God: the immanent, psychic God of the
third, subtle or celestial world called in Kabbala the "world of
formation." St. Peter recognized the immanent God of the soul.
By virtue of the divine presence in his soul, Peter saw and
believed. His was an act of faith, of affirmation. Eriugena
therefore says of Peter that he is the type of faith and action,
because these are the virtues of the soul. Indeed, we may say
that St. Peter is the soul, just as St. John is the spirit.

19

Faith is a new seed, "a grain of mustard seed," a first inchoate
movement of knowing in the soul, "an intellection of the heart,"
its morning star rising and day breaking. Eriugena writes, "Faith
is nothing else, in my opinion, but a certain principle from
which knowledge of the Creator begins to emerge in rational
nature." From faith, as from a seed, real knowledge unfolds by
metamorphosis; from faith, by fixation, real knowledge derives.
Faith has nothing to do with probability or hypothesis; it is not
a best bet; rather it is a kind of mystic certitude, "a firm
assurance of the things for which we hope," an unshakeable
conviction and confidence, a power that exists without rational
support. "I hold," wrote St. Gregory Palamas, "that our holy faith
. . . is a vision of our heart beyond all sensation and understanding."

   Faith, in other words, is the encounter of the human heart
with God — God's self-revelation in the human being. It is the
fulfillment of the prophecy of Jeremiah who foretold the great
turn when he wrote, "After those days, sayeth the Lord, I will put
my law in their inward parts, and will be their God, and they
shall be my people." This law, the Word which anoints in an
anointing which is the presence of the kingdom and the
kingdom of the presence, together with faith in the Word — the
Word's anointing — St. Augustine calls the interior master:

"Only the action of Christ in the heart allows the heart not to remain in solitude. Only the interior master teaches. Where anointing is absent, external words assail the ears to no avail."

Saving faith is the God within, the evidence in us of God's presence which makes possible our seeking of him. Seeking him in this way, we find ourselves truly and for the first time on our own home-ground. Guide and guided, lock and key, faith leads to and is our true nature. Beginning and end, seed and fruit, faith is the whole search, the uncovering of our original rootedness. It is not fidelity to law, nor any circumcision, but rather a deep opening in the heart of being — an opening which is also revelation: so that we may know.

As such, faith is a relationship which lives by love and will. For the soul must assent voluntarily to the heart's upspringing of love. Surrendering what is dead and arrested in us, what is living realizes itself in life, and God's immanence becomes one with his transcendence. When St. Peter, laying down "the old Adam," says, "Thou art the Son of the Living God," he recognizes and believes. Thereby a saving power, new knowledge by grace, is given to him. For Peter, faith thus becomes the substance of what he believes, at once superessential nourishment and the organ for its digestion. His faith in the Word becomes the Word's revelation in him.

Thereby faith becomes a sixth sense of spiritual sight. For, just as the ordinary world does not exist for one who cannot see, so the world of spiritual vision is without existence for one whose faith is unawakened. Faith, from this point of view, is the eye of the soul, the soul's awakening. As the soul's eye opens, the soul awakens. Faith, indeed, is the eye which must be open if the soul is to be awake. In a sense, faith is openness itself; yet it is an eye also which, as an eye, must not only be open and clear but also must be perpetually so. The eye of the soul, like the physical eye, must be self-clearing — transparent, virgin, image-free.

Therefore we may complement St. Peter with that other

paradigm of faith and the soul, Mary, who said, "Behold the handmaid of the Lord, be it unto me according to thy word." After all, it is Mary — rather than Moses or St. Peter — who most fully exemplifies the beginning of the Christian path of soul, for with her the contemplative life climaxes, not in any simple vision or knowledge of the divine, but in the very incarnation of the Word itself. Mary's faith is not simply psychic, but is bodily, of the whole person. She "circumscribed the corporeal in the incorporeal" in a wholly new way, giving birth to the body of the Word, who is the sanctifying wisdom of the world.

20

For Meister Eckhart, a virgin "designates a human being who is devoid of all foreign images and who is as void as he was when he was not yet." Such voidness, for Eckhart, is the active heart of faith. It is a kind of attention without an object, a silent waiting and openness. Traditionally it is said, "Faith cometh by hearing and hearing by the word of God." Such hearing is a dedicated listening, a devoted, silent attention. Above all, it is patient, an active, receptive passivity. It is to be without thoughts or images. If we stop thinking and patiently listen in silence we may hear the word spoken in silence: the word that silence speaks. "Listen closely to the instruction I am going to give you," Meister Eckhart says. "I could have so vast an intelligence that all the images human beings have ever received and those that are in God himself were comprehended in my intellect; however, if I were in no way attached to them, to the point that in everything I did or neglected to do, I did not cling to any of them with attachment — with its 'before' and 'after' — but in this present 'now' kept myself unceasingly free and void for the beloved will of God and its fulfillment, then should I indeed be a virgin, without the ties of all the images, as truly as I was when I was not yet."

This empty, waiting, receptive attention, this being without image and representation, is the sheer immediacy of pure experience: we may call it freedom, the fullness active beyond space and time. Through this smallest thing, a grain of mustard seed, the greatest is revealed and mountains are moved: the power of grace enters human reality and the kingdom, which is not of this world, is revealed. Now there are no categories rationally determined, no arbitrary labels. Observer and observed are one in the full supersensible flowering of what is. Habitual, reactive thinking ceases its movement, self-will its agony. Things speak in their autonomy. As Clement says, "Ordinary knowing is a state of mind that results from what is demonstrable, but faith is a grace which, from what is undemonstrated, conducts to what is universal and simple."

21

"Faith is one spirit with God," wrote Jacob Boehme, "for the Holy Spirit moves in the spirit of faith." Thus it is said of Mary, who is faith, that the Holy Spirit came upon her and the power of the Highest overshadowed her. Obediently waiting, she gave birth. Truly, emptiness of detachment gives birth to the Word of God in solitude. Opening to love, love opens; faith bears fruit, love is born. Therefore Evagrius of Pontus affirms:

> Love (*agape*) is the progeny of detachment (*apatheia*). Detachment is the very flower of discipline (*ascesis*). Discipline consists in keeping the commandments. The custodian of these commandments is the fear of God which is, in turn, the offspring of faith.

Faith, in other words, gives birth to the living recognition of God — St. Peter's affirmation — and brings about obedience, humility and selflessness. Thereby, by grace, detachment is born and, of detachment, love. Such love is the beginning of contemplation or higher knowledge, the first stage of which according to Evagrius is the contemplation of nature — *theoria physike*. This is the state in which phenomena become the symbols by whose activity in human souls the living truth of the Word is received. Nature and scripture alike become bearers of the good news. Ascending from this, Evagrius speaks finally of the height of contemplation, "first contemplation," which is the crown of love, the vision of the Holy Trinity in the Word. St. Peter therefore, as Eriugena represents him, finds himself just short of *apatheia* or detachment. For, as Evagrius says, "The perfect human being does not work at remaining continent, nor does the person with *apatheia* work at being patient."

22

Truly, faith is the seed whose fruit is the Word. But seed and fruit in a sense are one and so the Word is both the beginning and end of faith. In it is the beginning of the grace of self-discovery, whose end is to lose oneself in finding Him, oneself in Him. As the source of all human destiny, its ground and root, faith is necessarily the virtue of the soul or *anima*. Perfected by faith, this human soul and nature becomes the virgin vehicle for the Word's incarnation. Today, as sinners falling painfully short of the mark, we are rational creatures, for whom to think is to will and to represent, to oppose and to negate, to choose and to compare. Our spirit is one, as Goethe implied, that forever denies, or so it has become. We no longer know how to affirm or to embrace the world, for all our habits of mind, by which we understand the world, are exclusive and keep us tightly confined within the circle of what we already know. Hence the new and the holy can have no entrance for or in us; and we seem condemned to endure passively the nightmares of history. Faith, which is the entrance of the holy, must turn us around before we can awake. Negating itself, the negating power must be transformed. It must become other and open.

Rather than denying the Word, Peter should have denied himself. This is perhaps why tradition teaches that he was crucified head downwards. Like Peter, the soul must be turned upside down. This is the meaning of the faith which the Bible terms "repentance" which, in Greek, is *metanoia* or "change of mind (heart)." By repentance thinking becomes other than willing and representing. Renouncing these, and dissolving the categories of thought that rule us, we come to dwell in a different kind of thinking that Heidegger, following Meister Eckhart, calls "releasement." With this, the soul relinquishes its claims to be self-constituted and opens itself to the conscious-ness of things as they are in the Word. "O, how near God is to all things!" cries Jacob Boehme, adding: "Nevertheless, no thing can comprehend him unless it be tranquil and surrender to its own self-will. But if this is accomplished, then God acts through the instrumentality of everything, like the sun that acts through-out the whole world."

23

"What does it profit, my brethren, though a man say he hath faith, and have not works? Can faith save him?" asks St. James and answers, "Faith, if it hath not works, is dead. . . . For as the body without the spirit is dead, so faith without works is dead also." St. Peter, then, is not only the type of faith but also the type of works. He is the type of faith-and-action, action being the unfoldment and accomplishment of faith.

Action indeed is the living consummation of the directive implicit in faith. If faith is a seed, action is its germination and growth. The seed contains what it will become, but only as a potential. Without germination and the continuous presence of an appropriate medium, the seed becomes sterile, dead, a useless thing. Likewise faith without action is dead, for action is the germination of faith, whereby it comes to life in time and grows. Action, like the faith it enlivens, must therefore be continuous, for which reason we are enjoined to pray unceasingly. It is unceasing prayer — which is but another word for faith's activity — that leads faith to flower in knowledge and contemplation. Faith and action prepare the way for knowledge and contemplation, which they draw to themselves and grow into.

Hence the mystery of faith which St. Peter typifies in his meeting with the Son of the Living God has its other face in the "sacrament of contemplation" which St. John receives at Jesus's breast. The one is the counterpart of the other; together they constitute the fullness of human nature. As Eriugena said, "When we speak of the human mind, we discuss a single subject and do not double it ... except in respect of its functions." Contemplation is the ground and end of the path walked in faith and action. Like faith, whose prolongation it is, contemplation is a sacrament, a mystery conferring grace. It makes sacred and other, but it is not otherworldly. On the contrary, contemplation is the making manifest of the divine here and now, in the world.

An inclining love-filled grace is contemplation's ground: "Now, there was leaning on Jesus's breast one of his disciples whom Jesus loved. Simon Peter therefore beckoned to him that he should ask who it should be of whom he spake. He, then, lying on Jesus's breast, saith unto him, 'Lord, who is it?'" Jesus loves St. John and St. John, lying on his breast, open to the supernatural heart of his love, mediates between him and the other disciples, especially St. Peter who turns to him who is at home in the secret folds of Jesus's bosom to ask his questions and hear his answers.

In this relation John is to Jesus as Jesus is to the Father. St.

John leans on the bosom of Jesus while Jesus, the only begotten Son, is himself in the bosom of the Father, whence he declares him. As St. John is the means of St. Peter's questioning, so Jesus is the means of the Father's declaring. Furthermore, as Eriugena points out, the bosom of the Father is the Son. Resting on the Son's bosom, St. John rests on the bosom of the Father. No wonder, then, that he beholds the "countenance of the truth" directly, and not through any glass. Beholding the countenance of the truth, St. John is swept up into the substance of illumination and opened to the meaning that makes true things true. For true things may pass away, but truth — meaning — will never pass away. As St. Augustine says, "Truth remains even when true things perish."

Therefore the Word says, "Heaven and earth may pass away, but my words will never pass away." These immortal things, the words of the Word, are the primordial causes, the divine imaginations or logoi. Their mode of being is the Word's knowing. In God's Word, which is truth, are true immortal beings, prototypes of all things visible and invisible. Through these true words, also called "predestinations" and "wills," God makes — primordially and causally — all that he wishes to make. Hence truth, whose countenance profoundest contemplation grasps, is the principle of unity in the divine world. It is what ensures that causes and archetypes are not outside the divine but rather within it. And yet, paradox of paradoxes, truth is at the same time the openness of disclosure, the way whereby the divine-spiritual world reveals itself to itself in a vision of self-disclosure.

Confirming this, the Greek word for truth is *aletheia* — which means "unconcealment" or "un-forgetting." Hence we may say that truth is the divine reciprocation of the act of faith. For if faith is a radical openness, obedience, and receptivity, truth is the gift whereby openness reciprocates openness. The openness offered and that received are like a single beat. The one depends upon the other but in such complete freedom that relation is spiritual. There is only an identity of opposites because we as human beings lay ourselves down. We offer ourselves and in that faith we embrace the coming forward of what has retreated, the disclosing of what is concealed.

Between faith in the truth and truth's self-disclosure in grace, no creature intervenes. For as Eriugena repeatedly insists, following St. Augustine: "Between our minds, by which we understand the Father himself, and the truth, by which we understand him, there is no creature as intermediary." Truth, which is the disclosure of God, conforms to the openness whereby a human being knows God. Meister Eckhart refers to this when he writes, "The eye with which God sees me is the eye with which I see God, my eye and his are identical." More humbly, this is the experience of Coleridge when he observes that in his experience of the truth he seems "to will the truth, as well as to perceive it."

24

The openness of faith is nakedness, poverty; a stripping bare and a dying. Faith asks that we know ourselves existentially, to the bone. Knowing ourselves thoroughly, desires and attachments, hatreds and repulsions — everything that obstructs our present, immediate connection with reality — are transformed. When we no longer enclose them darkly but offer them to the transforming light and let them go, they let us go. Giving them their freedom, we receive our's. Therefore we must renounce all claim to possession, to what is past, even to ourselves, our own past; then, as the Sermon on the Mount says, the kingdom of heaven will open in us. Poverty of spirit, mourning, meekness, mercifulness, purity of heart, yearning for righteousness, persecution — such are the stations of faith.

Such faith is a kind of crucifixion. Eriugena paraphrasing St. Maximus, his master in the spiritual life, writes:

For each of the faithful, in whatever measure he possesses
the constitution of soul in order to increase in virtue, to
that degree his faith in Christ receives an increase of
intelligence. And as often as he dies to his earlier and lower
way of life, and is carried to a higher level, all his beliefs
about Christ, however simple, die in and within him, and
are carried by faith and intelligence to ever more sublime
theophanies. Thus Christ dies daily with his faithful, and is
crucified by them, while they destroy their sense-bound
and still spiritually imperfect cognitions of him, and in this
way they ascend ever higher until they attain true knowledge of him, for the infinite is formed by the infinite even
in the most purified minds.

In other words, faith is creative metamorphosis, perpetual
transformation. Casting off body, soul, and even spirit, one dies
to each in turn. This is the movement of faith-action-knowledge-
contemplation-deification, a continuous dying of what is dead
so that what is living can come to life.

This movement continuously breaks down the fixed categories that reduce our lives to a kind of automatism; it breaks
down the blocks, the endless series of arrests that confine us to
a living death, a life of the tomb, from which the rock has not
yet rolled away. Faith rolls the rocks away, gives us wings, lets
us soar.

25

Mary Magdalene, human nature in its faithful turning-around,
having come early and alone, when it was still dark, saw *the
stone taken away from the tomb*, and ran to tell Simon Peter
and the disciple whom Jesus loved, "They have taken the Lord
out of the tomb and we know not where they have laid him."
Faith and intellect — Peter and John — therefore set out
together, knowing that everything rests on what they will find,
for as St. Paul says, "If Christ be not risen, then your faith is vain."

The tomb is critical. It is the central initiatory metaphor of the Christian path, the cardinal point of its orientation. Occupied, it marks the fullness of the Word's surrender; empty, it marks his resurrection. Between these two moments lies the mysterious intersection of life and death, natural and supernatural, human and divine — two states, once separable, now indivisible. The Crucified is the Risen, the Risen is the Crucified. In this simultaneity and identity lies the mystery of the tomb, the good news of redemption.

Here redemption is that of human nature suffering in the tomb of the world, Plato's cave of death and illusion. This tomb-cave is the tomb-body (*soma-sema*) of a fallen world, its fallen body, the fallen body of the universe — so that it is not just the redemption of humanity that is at issue, but the redemption of the universe as a whole. Its emptiness marks the redemption of all things, not just human beings. "All of creation groaned and travailed in pain until now." Christianity thus proposes not just a way but the active redemption of the universe in its totality. Uncovering the empty tomb begins the journey home, humanity bearing within it the seed of cosmic spiritualization.

The Word's embrace of the fullness of birth and death, his permeation of the tomb or charnel house of the world, turns cosmic winter into spring. "Everywhere the universe sings, Alleluia!" The tomb-world is empty, overcome. Death is no more. Redemption is everywhere. Supernatural flowers shoot to the sky. "Why mourn and seek your buried Lord?" sings Eriugena:

> Death is defeated, behold your God in joy!
> Stop thinking you see gardeners' faces —
> The Lord is living! Whom you mourn: behold!

This is the reality: the risen Word is present now. In each of the Gospels Christ appears by the empty tomb, and in each instance his message is the same: "Why seek you the living

among the dead? He is not here but is risen." Feel his presence!
The empty tomb is not past or future, but the present moment,
pure spontaneity, improvisation. That is the meaning of resurrection. In the words of Emil Bock: "Christian devotion has
ultimately no other purpose than this: to cherish community
with the Risen Christ. Christ is not to be sought either in the
past or in the future, but in the immediate present. His sphere
is not a beyond; he is near to us in the world in which we live."

Only an illusory membrane separates this world from that
— only a moment of turning. Such is the tomb, at once so little
and so much. "No one is saved by the death of Christ if he is not
born of the spirit," writes Eriugena, adding, "no one is born of
the spirit if it is not in the death of Christ." This is the traditional
doctrine. In St. Paul's words, "We are buried with him by
baptism unto death; that, like as Christ was raised from the dead
by the glory of the Father, even so we should walk in newness
of life."

Death — the tomb — is the womb of new life. Truly, the
birth in the cave of the manger and the death and resurrection
in the cave of the tomb constitute a single line of redemption in
which tomb and womb are like two beats of one heart.
Therefore the Greek Liturgy proclaims (of the birth, but it could
as well have been of the baptism or of the empty tomb), "The
wall of separation has been dissolved, the flaming sword has
turned back, and the Cherubim have moved away from the Tree
of Life, and I partake of the life of Paradise. . . . Today the Virgin
gives birth to the Maker of the universe. *The cave brings forth
Eden.*"

Concealed here in the cave-tomb of birth-death is the
mystic heart, the heart of the world in the cave of the heart, the
supreme place, the hidden center, the dwelling-place of the
divine. Thus Agni in Hindu thought, the Cosmic Fire, supports
the universe and abides in the secret place of the heart: *nihitam
guhayam*, literally 'hidden in the cave.' This Agni is *Atma*
which, according to the *Chandogya Upanisad*, "dwells in the

heart, is smaller than a grain of barley, smaller than a grain of mustard, smaller than a grain of millet, smaller than the germ which is in the grain of millet." And yet this smallest of things is also "greater than the earth, greater than the atmosphere, greater than the sky, greater than all the worlds together."

Hereby tomb and cave, heart and kingdom, are brought together with faith. For this *Atma* in the cave of the heart is none other than the kingdom which is, and is opened by, faith. For Jesus speaks in almost the same words of both. Of the kingdom, he says: "This kingdom is like unto a grain of mustard seed, which a man took and sowed in his field: which indeed is the least of all seeds; but when it is grown, it is the greatest among herbs, and become a tree, so that the birds of the air come and lodge in the branches thereof." Of faith, he says: "If ye have faith as a grain of mustard seed, ye shall say unto this mountain, remove to yonder place; and it shall remove; and nothing shall be impossible to you."

Thus the tomb is the entry into divine life, which is infinite, by means of faith, which is original human nature, the least and greatest of all things. This is the tomb blocked by the great stone or letter of the sense world.

26

In his commentary on St. John the Baptist's saying "He it is who, coming after me, is preferred before me, whose shoe's latchet I am not worthy to unloose," Eriugena writes:

> One may say that Christ's shoes signify visible creation and scripture, for in these he has fixed his traces as though with his feet. Visible creation is truly the garment of the Word since, manifesting his beauty to us, it makes him known openly; and sacred scripture has also become his garment because it contains his mysteries. Of these two realities — creation and scripture — the precursor considers

himself not worthy to unloose the latchet, that is, the subtlety. The two feet of the Word are, on the one hand, the natural *ratio* of visible creation and, on the other, the spiritual meaning of sacred scripture. The first is cloaked by the sensible forms of the sensible world, the second by the outer shell of the divine letters, that is, by sacred scripture. In two ways, then, have commentators on the Divine Law unveiled the incarnation of the Word of God. According to the first they teach that he was incarnated in the Virgin, joining himself to human nature in the unity of his substance. According to the other they assert that this same Word is as if incarnated, that is, thickened, by letters and by the shapes and lines of visible things. The latchet of this double shoe, which the precursor felt himself unworthy to unloose, is diligent research and minute investigation of the truth in this twofold manner.

Just as being born of a virgin the Word became flesh, so too he incarnated in the letters of scripture and the varied forms of the visible universe. St. Anthony, the Desert Father, when asked, "How do you ever manage to carry on, deprived as you are of the consolation of books?" replied, "My book, sir philosopher, is the nature of created things, and that is always at hand when I wish to read the words of God." Thus there is an equivalence, almost an identity, between nature and scripture. The Word is equally present in both and both are in equal measure words of God. Both are signs or gestures evoking principles. Both evoke meaning and permit its realization.

Implicit here is the sacramental view that all knowledge is revelation, a perfectly modulated interpenetration of humanity and grace, nature and supra-nature. To the person in the Word, in whom the Word is the person, the Word in the universe speaks. He speaks in the heart. Mountain, grasses, and trees become his Gospels, clouds and animals his prophets. What then impedes this marvelous development, the flowering of meaning and understanding in the Word. Nothing else than the stone which, though rolled away, still seems to block the tomb.

The besetting danger is idolatry, the sin of the reification of the letter, the worship of the weight and density of literality. This weight must be removed, just as the stone was from the tomb. Likewise the idea of "objectivity" and "representation" must be removed before nature can speak in its authentic spiritual tongue. Otherwise one lives in "a desert of idolatry," like the one where John the Baptist preached and Christ came to be baptized. For, according to Eriugena, the Jews of that time were "contaminated by all the infamies of idolatry, addicted only to the letter of the law — to a letter devoid of all spiritual meaning and polluted by all kinds of superstition." But that is not only an historical description. It is still true today and we are all "Jews of that time." Superstition, idolatry, literality — these are forms of materialism and alienation we know only too well. All stem from taking the shadow for the reality. Truly, this world is still the tomb of Plato's cave. We live in it in a world of shadows under the tyranny of the letter, confined to the sense-perceptible as to a tomb. But, rising to the spiritual meaning, the stone is rolled away, shadows dissipate, light floods in.

27

For Eriugena, the letter is synonymous with the law. Both are "the shadow and symbol" of the spirit. Not evil in themselves, they are but a partial good, and as such dangerous and misleading. Indeed, considered in their nakedness, disconnected from the whole, letter and law are interchangeably instruments of coercion: they are heavy, they oppress and set up opposition and duality. Yet, in the Word, they are truth and grace. The discontinuity is absolute. Two worlds that only a third, faith, can bridge.

Just as Adam and Eve, after they had eaten of the fruit of the Tree of Good and Evil — comparative knowledge — immediately *saw* that they were naked and were ashamed at the sudden and irreducible otherness that had come upon them, so too the nakedness of law and letter irrevocably sets these up as opposed, autonomous, and sufficient unto themselves.

How then is this weight to be lifted? In St. Matthew's Gospel, "There was a great earthquake.... The angel of the Lord descended from heaven and rolled back the stone." The other Gospels are less explicit. The disciples simply come to the tomb and find the stone rolled away. This is one of the mysteries of faith, that it can move mountains. Faith, which is the substance of prayer, as in the saying, "Ask, and it shall be given you; seek, and ye shall find; knock, and it shall be opened unto you," this faith is the organ for truth and grace. Without it, in the reduced world of law and letter, two demonic temptations constantly arise: arrogance and despair. Arrogance would set up human ego-consciousness as a law unto itself, the sole and self-constituted creator of its world; while despair, rightly rejecting this possibility, falls into the bleak nihilism of believing that humanity can know, be, and achieve nothing beyond the sensible world. These two positions constitute the logical end of idolatry. Truth and grace alone are their cure.

Consider the feeding of the five thousand. The question is how to feed the mass of ordinary people. A young boy — mystically, Moses, the legislator, here called a "boy" because "he prefigures the unity of the future church" — has five barley loaves and two fishes. In his *Commentary*, Eriugena writes:

> The five barley loaves are the five books of the Mosaic Law which are rightly called 'barley' because they nourish carnal knowledge. In fact, properly speaking, barley is the food of beasts of burden, not of humans. Carnal humanity, which still lives beneath the yoke of the letter has not yet abandoned the age of the first person of whom it was written, 'he is compared to the beasts that have no understanding and is like them,' — carnal humanity is reckoned among the beasts and is therefore fed, not with the spiritual marrow of the letter, but with the letter alone, as with barley bread with which straw has been mixed. Indeed, barley grain sticks naturally to the straw husks, so

that the marrow can scarcely be separated from it, which is why barley grains signify the difficulty of spiritually apprehending not only sensible signs but also the precepts of the law. The number five, which is the number of the barley loaves, is also appropriately understood as indicating the five senses. Truly, to whatever extent one of the faithful delights in what is received through the senses — to that extent must he be reckoned among the beasts. If, on the contrary, living and growing in both action and knowledge, he is nourished by spiritual meat — then he is no longer to be numbered among the beasts, but may be counted among rational creatures.... But no one would know how to rise to heights of virtue and contemplation if he were not first fed by tokens of sensible things. And so the Lord distributes loaves of barley bread to the crowds following him so that, once filled, these faithful souls should be led to higher, spiritual foods of rational creatures. But by these they cannot be nourished until they have transcended their corporeal senses and all that they have received through them....

To feed the five thousand, Jesus asks them to sit down. At this point the text adds, "Now, there was much grass in that place," signifying, according to Eriugena, "the letter of the law." It is described as "much" because of the many carnal thoughts introduced into the soul by the senses. Nevertheless, in order to eat, the people must sit on the grass — for the way to the Word begins "in the simplicity of the letter and visible creation." Eriugena explains: "The first stage in the ascension of virtues is the letter of sacred scripture and the species of visible things. One must first read the letter of scripture and observe creation, in order to rise by right thinking to the spirit of the letter and the *ratio* (or logos) of creation." No one, indeed, may rise to heights of virtue and contemplation unless he is first nourished by the symbolism of sensible things, "the world of visible sacraments and sensible creatures." And so the five thousand, who symbolize "the fullness of those who live according to the flesh but who, once taught by sacred history and the observation of visible things, may arrive at the heights of spiritual things," are seated upon the grass. Jesus then takes loaves and fishes and, giving thanks, distributes them — that is, "distinguishes their visible signs from their invisible meanings, and apportions these according to the capacity of each to receive." Then, everyone having eaten his fill, he asks the disciples to gather up what is left: twelve basketsful. Thereby the mass of simple but faithful souls is shown to be satisfied with the letter alone, for the fragments that remain — a vast quantity — are the spiritual meanings that human beings in their carnality cannot consume. Therefore "the Masters of the Church receive the order to gather them, so that none of these spiritual meanings should be lost because of never having been assimilated by spiritual intelligence."

The letter, then, which is sense-perception that has not been raised up into the Word, is the first stage to higher knowledge. Without it, indeed, there is no spiritual knowledge for incarnated beings. But its weight must be removed. It must be penetrated, raised up, made transparent. The objectified and objectifying I must be cast off. Then this weight becomes grace and truth — which tells us *who* has done the rolling aside and casting off and *who* now does the seeing.

28

The weight of the letter being lifted, the tomb is opened. St. John, knowledge and contemplation, more deeply purified, arrives first. St. Peter, faith and action, not yet fully purified, follows. And enters first, for faith is always the beginning. Not that it is simply a preparation for knowledge, something to be used in its place and then set aside. On the contrary, faith is a permanent state, a continuing and growing precondition and synthesis of what it heralds. In this sense it is the rock of certitude formed into the house being built upon it. *Fides quaerit*, faith seeks; *intellectus invenit*, intellect finds. Spirit embraces and crowns faith seeking it. But faith opens the way — faith, which is the human soul enters first; then intelligence follows, the spirit descends.

The comparison between St. Peter and St. John has a deeper foundation, for Peter and John stand not only for two stages of the spiritual path but also for two relations to the Word, two Christologies — i.e., two stages in the human understanding of divinity. The question of who Christ is, which is the question of the Trinity, is the central Christian question. Is Jesus simply the "anointed," God's representative, or is he God as such, absolutely and totally the absolute unknowable Creator and Ground of all things that are and are not? Who or what is he? An angel? A man of god-consciousness? Or God as such?

How is one to meet and know the Word? For Christians this is the central question. All St. John's writings are dedicated to creating a context in which the highest, purest, deepest answer can emerge. For this reason he is called the "Theologian," for among the Gospel writers only he rose to the point of plainly declaring (as Origen put it) the Godhead of the Word. St. Mark, for instance, does not confess Jesus to be the Son of God until after the crucifixion; in St. Matthew, St. Peter only recognizes Jesus as the one anointed by the Living God. St. John alone knows Christ from the start as the pre-existent Word, maker of the world, life and light of human beings, forever united with the divine ground of the Father, his name and only begotten Son. But more than this, St. John affirms this same Word to be the savior of the world, made flesh and dwelling amongst us, not different from us. That is to say, he affirms the double reality of the Word in the Godhead and the Word made flesh, seen and touched. He proclaims not just the divinity of the Word but the spiritualization and sanctification of "matter" as a consequence of the Word's assumption of the flesh by his birth, death, and resurrection. St. Peter does not go so far. He meets Christ and knows him to be a living power. He resonates with him. But he is not changed; he remains the same: stubborn, headstrong, egotistic, wavering. But St. John is changed utterly. Become love, which is knowledge *and* flesh, he radiates sanctifying compassion forever.

29

Origen writes of St. John's Gospel:

> No one can apprehend the meaning of it, except he hath lain on Jesus' breast and received from Jesus Mary to be his mother also. Such a one must he become who is to be another John and to have shown to him, like John, by Jesus himself, Jesus as he is. For if Mary, as those with sound mind declare, had no other son but Jesus, and yet Jesus says to her [of John], "Woman, behold thy son," and not, "Behold, you have this son also," then he virtually says to her, "Lo, this is Jesus whom thou didst bear." Is it not the case that everyone who is perfect no longer lives for himself, but Christ lives in him? And if Christ lives in him is it not said of him to Mary, "Behold, thy son Christ."

All of which is to say not only that John, entering into the paradise of paradises, is deified, but also that in becoming so he does not achieve anything that is not his and our natural human birthright. For although all created natures are alienated from the uncreated nature of God, all are by nature called to be "partakers of the divine." Only the Word is the only begotten Son, but by virtue of his incarnation all creatures without exception are now also called to become children of God by participation or adoption — to be penetrated by divinity as a red-hot iron is penetrated by fire. God in the end *must* appear as he is: all in all. Thus Eriugena writes: "Just as air appears to be wholly light and melted iron wholly fiery ... so a sound intellect will realize that after the end of this world every nature remaining intact will seem to be God alone." It is a remarkable paradox that God "who cannot be apprehended in himself" is apprehended in a certain way through creation, while creation itself, by an ineffable miracle, is transformed into God. This miracle is *deification*, the crown of wisdom, the very summit of contemplation. This is the full realization of the Word-born fruit of the incarnation, the Word himself. As Eriugena says, "The fruit of the Tree of Life, Christ, is a blessed life, eternal peace in contemplation of the truth, which is properly called deification."

Here we plunge into the deepest secrets of theology and anthropology, where ordinary thinking loses its footing and the impossible becomes possible. That is why these ideas are so little known and, though basic, are only obscurely part of our cultural beliefs and values. This is not new. It already puzzled Eriugena, who wrote: "The word 'deification' is rarely found in Latin books, but its meaning is found in many authors, especially Ambrose. Perhaps it is that the meaning of the word *theosis*, commonly used by the Greeks to signify the passing of saints into God not only in soul but also in body, when nothing animal, corporeal, human or natural remains in them — perhaps, I say, to those unable to rise above carnal thoughts it seems too lofty, incomprehensible and incredible, and hence not to be proclaimed in public."

And yet, deification is central to Christian cosmology. It is the end for which humanity and the cosmos were created, for the purpose of creation is union with God, that God should be all in all. "Let us become gods through the Lord," exclaims St. Maximus, "because for this did humanity come to exist: God and Master by nature." Such is human destiny for, in Eriugena's words, "Just as each and everything, whether sensible or intelligible, is naturally compelled to return to its beginnings, so human nature also will return to its beginning, which is nothing other than God's Word, in which it was made, and unchangeably subsists and lives."

But the will, the means of attachment to divinity, has turned aside. Humanity, synonymous with cosmos, perfect in itself and incorruptible — in other words, synonymous also with paradise — has fallen and became unnatural. All its functions are now corrupted; the natural order is overturned. Sin and death rule. Isolation and opposition take the place of union and identity. Denying freedom — Adam blaming Eve and Eve blaming the serpent — human nature falls into unfreedom. Yet God's plan does not change. It is still and forever his unchanging desire and certain knowledge that his image and likeness shall be all in all. This human nature is never not called for deification.

The incarnation of the Word, no end in itself, is the means to this. The divine obedience, the perfect freedom, of the second Adam and the second Eve makes possible the fulfillment of the original plan, now revealed under the aspect of universal salvation and cosmic transfiguration. "Redemption" thus is but the negative of the divine affirmation; and atonement, rendered necessary by sin, is not an end but a means. Even salvation itself is therefore a negative moment, for the essential reality remains union with God.

God, the uncreated, assumed human nature, the created, in order that the created might become the uncreated — in order that human nature might become divine. This was the Good News that startled and transfixed the early Fathers:

> an ineffable descent *katabasis*
> a divine self-emptying *kenosis*
> an ascent *anabasis*
> a deification *theosis*
> and a final restoration *apocatastasis*

By God's own submission to the flesh and death, to hell and resurrection, the obstacle of sin was removed. By the incarnation, humanity and divinity, created and uncreated natures, were reconciled — but without any violation to the freedom of created nature. On the contrary, the incarnation restored the very freedom that is created nature.

Commenting on Jesus' saying to Nicodemus, "No man hath ascended up to heaven, but he that came down from heaven, even the Son of man which is in heaven," Eriugena writes:

> As to his ascending and descending, Christ himself clearly explains what these are when he says, "I came forth from the Father, and am come into the world, again I leave the world and go to the Father." His coming forth from the Father is his assumption of human nature; his return to the Father is his deification of the human nature that he assumed and the raising of it to the very heights of divinity. He came down alone, since he incarnated alone. But as to whether he ascends alone, what may those for whom he descended believe? Their hope is great and inexplicable, for all those are saved who ascend in him, now faith and hope, and at the end of time face to face and in reality. For this is what John writes in his Epistle when he says, "Now we are sons of God, and it doth not yet appear what we shall be; but we know that when he shall appear, we shall be like him and know him as he is." Thus he came forth alone, and he returned alone, because with all his members he is the one God, the only son of God. All those who truly believe in him are one with him. Christ alone, body and members, went to the Father. . . .

Through the incarnation all natures are adopted as sons of God and are opened to deification by their participation in the Word's unity with his father. Thus the Word reveals the sons of God hidden from the beginning in human nature. Nor must we ever forget that human nature is nature as such — that humanity is the cosmos. The gathering, restoration and deification includes not only humanity but all of creation, visible and invisible.

By the assumption of humanity, the Word makes possible the deification of this universe, this life, now. St. John proclaims this possibility, leaving a record of it not only in his Gospel but also in his Epistles and his Apocalypse. Paraphrasing St. Gregory Palamas, we may say that St. John, participating in the divine energy, became light in himself. Light united to light, in and through the light and with all his faculties he beheld the secrets of the Word. In the words of Palamas, "Thus he surpasses not only the corporeal senses, but also all that can be known." Or, as St. Maximus put it, in a passage translated by Eriugena, "While remaining in his soul and body entirely human by nature, he becomes in his soul and body entirely God by grace, by the divine splendor of the beatifying glory which is wholly expedient for him."

Not only does the Word take part in this act of deification, but also the whole Trinity is present, as Eriugena makes clear in the following quotation:

> The Father is light, fire, heat; the Son is light, fire, heat; and the Holy Spirit is light, fire, heat. The Father enlightens, the Son enlightens, the Holy Spirit enlightens, for from them all knowledge and wisdom are given. The Father burns, the Son burns, the Holy Spirit burns, because they consume our sins together, and by *theosis* — i.e., by deification — they convert us, as though we were a holocaust, into their unity. Just so, the Father heats, the Son heats, and the Holy Spirit heats, because with one and the same surging tide of love they foster and nourish us. As though from the deformity of our imperfection after the fall of the first human being, they bring us up to the perfect human being, and train us for the fullness of Christ's time.

Thus St. John, deified, entered the one cause of all and heard the one Word through which all things were made.

As for his deification, clearly if he had not been first transmuted into God, he could not have known God, for only like may know like. "Never did eye see the sun, unless it had first become sunlike, and never can the soul have vision of the first beauty unless it itself be beautiful," wrote Plotinus, echoing a tradition at least as old as Empedocles. However, to become

sunlike the eye must already have something of the sun about it.
As Goethe says, "If the eye were not of the sun's essence, how
could it ever perceive the sun? If the divine spark were not
native to us, how could it move us to rapture?" In other words,
If the soul were not godlike by nature, how could it ever
become godlike by grace?

St. John, revealing the highest and the holiest, becomes a
divine messenger, an angel and interpreter of God and god-
likeness. Ascending Jacob's ladder, he knows and declares the
Word in the beginning; descending it, he knows and declares
that same Word made flesh. Made an angel, St. John, renouncing
himself and all he is, lives in God, a discarnate teacher. Of such
angels, Sergei Bulgakov wrote: "Incorporeal spirits, pure subsis-
tences in their free love renounce their selfhood; they live only
outside themselves, not their own life; in their metaphysical
self-emptying they are in their very nature only angels, impersonal *metaxu*, mere go-betweens." Such St. John became in the
Word, but not entirely, for, paradoxically, he remained himself.

30

St. John, therefore, surpassing the mountain peak of theology
and contemplation, dwelling in the Word and indwelt by it,
became one with supreme transcendent connectedness and
relation of all, the Blessed Trinity. Travelling the infinite way, he
passed from his interiority into God's and entered the threefold
inner life of the Godhead. There he apprehended mystically the
eternal circulating play of the Father, the Word, and the Holy
Spirit. For the Father's Word goes out from him and returns to
him in his Spirit. Indeed, this Father, the fountain of all powers,
the source and self-subsisting principle of all fullness and
emptiness — this Father bursts forth in his Word who is his
name and his heart and who, the cause of all, gathers all up in
joy, shining in the Father as the Father shines in him. This Father

and this Word live in the Father's Spirit, who is the body of the Godhead, its full completion and inner reality, the light of its life. It is to this that St. Paul refers when he invokes, "One God and Father of all, who is above all, and through all, and in you all": *Above all* is the Father, the divine source; *through all* is the Word, the wisdom of I AM; and *in you all* is the Spirit, the divine interiority of living relation, the pure activity and divine immanence of love. This ternary groundless ground and infinite connectedness Eriugena, for his part, names "the secret of the one Essence in the three Substances and the three Substances in the one Essence."

In the second chapter of *The Divine Names*, called "Concerning the Undifferencing and Differentiation in Divinity and the nature of Divine Unification and Differentiation," Dionysius the Areopagite writes: "All the names proper to God are always applied in scripture not partially but to the whole, entire, full, complete Godhead, and refer indivisibly, absolutely, unreservedly, and wholly to the wholeness of the whole entire Godhead." To divide or number the deity, then, is obvious blasphemy; and yet, Dionysius continues, "Sacred science sometimes employs a method of Undifference and sometimes one of Differentiation," adding that "we must never disjoin those things which are undifferenced nor confuse those things which are differentiated."

Undifferenced names belong to the Godhead without distinction or qualification. They include both "negative" designations (such as "super-excellent," "super-essential," "super-divine") and positive, causal titles such as good, beautiful, true, wise, life-giving, etc. These undifferenced names — "hidden, incommunicable ultimates" — describe a single divine nature and are indefinite in number and inexhaustible in possibility. *Differentiated* names, on the other hand, are starkly and simply limited to three — Father, Son and Holy Spirit — which are neither interchangeable nor held in common, but rather indicate *relations of absolute, radical difference.* The Father is not the Son, the Son is not the Holy Spirit, nor is the Holy Spirit the Father: each is different and other. These three have always been three, and always will be, for their threeness is inevitable and eternal. As Gregory of Nazianzen writes:

> If there was a time when the Father was not, then there was a time when the Son was not. If there was a time when the Son was not, then there was a time when the Spirit was not. If the one was from the beginning, then the three were too. If you throw down one, I am bold to assert that you do not set up the other two. For what profit is there in an imperfect Godhead?

Each of these three is different and unique. Contemplation of the one cause reveals it not to be barren but to possess in infinite fertility three movements in one nature, three relations in a single silent void. Whoever invokes one simultaneously invokes the other two for these three are undivided and indivisibly united. "When I speak of God, you must be illumined by one flash of light and by three," wrote St. Gregory, confessing, "No sooner do I conceive of the One than I am illumined by the splendor of the Three; no sooner do I distinguish them, than I am carried back to the One." And yet: "The Son is not the Father, because there is only one Father, but the Son is what the Father is; the Holy Spirit, though he proceeds from the Father, is not the Son, because there is only one only begotten Son, but the Holy Spirit is what the Son is." To arrive at a formulation of this irreducibility, which is nonconceptual, required, as Vladimir Lossky says, "the superhuman efforts of an Athanasius of Alexandria, of a Basil, of a Gregory Nazianzen." These Greek fathers transformed an impoverished dialectic into the full apophatic richness of the Trinity. God is one and three. This simple reality prevents the all too human mind from objectifying the divine Essence outside of the Divine Persons and their eternal circulation in love.

It is indeed only in their circulation that they may be

known. Each is unique, but outside of their relations we may know nothing of them. Eriugena writes of St. Gregory that "when he was questioned by the Eunomians concerning this name of Father, whether it signified a nature or an operation, enlightened by divine grace, [he] made a wonderful reply, saying that it was the name neither of a nature nor of an operation, but only of *the relation to the Son.*" The name of the Son likewise is only the name of a relation; as also is the name of the Holy Spirit. There are thus three relations. In Eriugena's formulation: the state of the Unbegotten substance in relation to the Begotten; the state of the Begotten in relation to the Unbegotten; and the state of the Proceeding in relation to the Unbegotten and the Begotten. Three relations, interrelated as source, generation, and procession; three determinations of one absolute essence; three manifestations of the only Self. Nicholas of Cusa will call these relations unity, equality, and connection, for unity must be equal and connected with itself. If there is otherness, as the Father is other than his Word, so there must be sameness, harmony, and connectedness. Such is the mysterious Tri-Unity, a supernumber that can be expressed in no other way nor understood in any other form: "a unity that cannot be divided, a tri-unity that cannot but be distinguished" (Coleridge). As Evagrius of Pontus wrote: "The Holy Trinity is a unique essence and essential knowledge."

The Trinity is not a number; it is not preceded by a Dyad, nor followed by a Tetrad. It is not constituted by addition. God cannot be numbered; he is simply and identically One and Three. Thus St. John distinguishes but does not divide Father and Son, Beginning and Word. But here a question arises. Plunged as he is into the very *arcanum* of the one Cause of all, St. John, distinguishing Beginning and Word, should immediately and simultaneously pass onto the third distinction, for it is impossible for him to distinguish Two without Three. But where is the Third, the Holy Spirit? No explicit mention seems to be made of it.

Not surprisingly, the Holy Spirit has always been the most obscure member of the Holy Trinity. And yet, just as the Son inhumated in outward, visible form, and thereby entered the stream of earthly-human history and time, so too the Holy Spirit is said to be active, working invisibly and inwardly in terrestrial life. Indeed, the fact of the incarnation means that Word and Spirit now reveal themselves and the Father. Both are with us now, as the Father's presence — his spirit and his wisdom. Before the incarnation, the Father was not yet known as the Father; the divine Persons were not clearly distinguished for human consciousness. But of course they existed. God was always Three — but his Threeness was hidden. Or rather: it had become hidden. Before the Fall the Trinity was always present. But after the Fall the Three withdrew into a nameless, transcendent cloud. God spoke, breathed his breath upon his people, but his Word could not be fully understood. It could not be heard or grasped directly. It had to be taken on faith, and for generations human being struggled to recall, to hear. Thus they developed new strengths of memory and consciousness. Then, suddenly, gratuitously, full utterance spoke forth, complete recall was possible: the Word was made flesh, again.

Here is the mystery: this most extraordinary event occurred, and could only have occurred, through the double action of the Divine in concert with human nature. For the Father incarnates his only Son, the Word, in human flesh with the aid, not only of the purifying, conceiving fire of the Holy Spirit, but also of the pure, compliant conception of the Blessed Virgin. Within her womb the first fruits were formed. Simply put, in the words of a Greek mystic, Nicholas Cabasilas: "The Incarnation was not only the work of the Father, by his Power and his Spirit, it was also the work of the will and the faith of the Virgin. Without the consent of the Immaculate, without the agreement of her faith, the plan was as unrealizable as it was without the intervention of the Three Divine Persons themselves." Who, then, is this Virgin, in and by whom the incarnation was made possible? How to distinguish her, and thereby human nature, whose perfect representative she is, from Word and Spirit?

Certainly, she is central, this Mother of God, "the source and root of the races of liberty." Obtaining gifts for human beings and angels, she is the channel of grace, "the habitation of the infinite." What a paradox she is! Though not herself infinite, she is able to contain infinity! This is her special mark — that she lives between two worlds, adorning both of them. In a sense, she has already become what humanity is destined to be, for she lives in the Word, passing on his gifts from on high. This is the problem — usually it is the Holy Spirit who is the giver and gift of grace, but in practice, in the experience of these last Christian centuries, it is often Mary who plays that role. And who can tell them apart? As grace, the Holy Spirit is a descent, but a descent is impossible without an ascent, something risen to receive it. Rising becomes descending, descending rising. Who can tell them apart in this dance of created and uncreated? Who is the dancer, who the dance?

From earliest time, the sphere of the Spirit's activity — which is sanctification — and its object — which is human nature — have been inextricably intertwined: intertwined as divine and human in the Word, as body, soul, and spirit in the human being. All these, though distinguishable, are indivisible. The one is in the other; they reciprocate in perpetual cycles of reciprocation, and cannot be taken apart. Without Mary, without humanity, the Word's revelation of the Trinity would have remained purely spiritual. Without a divine-human conception, without the circumincession of divine and human love, this universe would have remained forever in barren desolation. But through Mary and human nature, the light shines in the darkness and the universe is glorified with the presence of God.

Where, then, is the Holy Spirit if not in the very fact of St. John's being able to enter into the *arcanum* and there proclaim the beginning and the Word? Where else, indeed, than in the very proclamation itself? A proclamation that is the living synthesis of St. John's humanity and the gift of knowledge accorded him. St. John begins his Gospel by virtue of an ability which is a gift — a gift of the Holy Spirit, by whose wings of grace the voice of the Eagle strikes in the hearing of the church. But not only of the Holy Spirit, for it is St. John's human nature that is his voice.

This nature, whose perfected representative is Mary, is like St. John the *anima* without whose faithful and detached obedience the *animus* or spirit may not descend, nor the human person partake of eternal life.

According to St. Maximilian Kolbe, who was given the life-task of solving the riddle posed by the Virgin at Lourdes when she said, *I am the Immaculate Conception*: "Ordinarily, everything comes from the Father through the Son and by the Holy Spirit; and everything returns by the Holy Spirit through the Son to the Father." Ordinarily, that is, the Father is the source, the Son is the only begotten from the beginning, and the Holy Spirit is "the flowering of the love of the Father and the Son." This is the traditional view of the Roman Church, but St. Maximilian goes further, saying: "If the fruit of created love is a created conception, then the fruit of divine love, that prototype of all created love, is necessarily a 'divine conception' ... an infinitely holy 'immaculate conception.'" For St. Maximilian, the Mother of God is a creature, but she is God's most perfect creature. She is the most perfect image of God and the most filled with him. Indeed, she is the *spouse* of the Holy Spirit, united with the Holy Spirit in ineffable union and a single life — a union so close that we cannot grasp it. This union is "the summit of love." In it, "heaven and earth meet, all of heaven with all of earth, the totality of divine eternal love with the plenitude of created love."

Such are the wings upon which the Eagle soars, beyond mind and body, the wings of the Holy Spirit, the wings of love.

PART TWO: THE WORD
(*Homily*: Chapters VI–XIII)

1

"Eternity is the very substance of our God," says St. Augustine, while Tatian, one of the earliest Christian writers, claims, "Our God did not begin to be in time. He alone is without beginning and he himself is the beginning of all things." All of which is to say, as St. Basil does, that the beginning of time is but "the rapid and imperceptible moment of creation" which, instantaneous and indivisible, is not itself time, nor even the least particle of it, any more than the beginning of a road is a road, or the beginning of a house is a house. Creation, the act of which is eternal and continuous, is rather the seed of time, its ever-present synthesis and possibility. It exists outside temporal consciousness, which is as it were at once its death and its trace and prolongation. *In the beginning was the Word*, therefore, must be understood neither temporally nor spatially, but as referring to the creative source of all. It must not be associated with time in any sense of temporal duration but with eternity, for passing time is one thing and the present moment is another, ever-present reality whose whole content is "an immediate concentration with itself" (Plotinus). It exists as the announcement of identity in the divine, of that state — of being thus and not otherwise — which characterizes what has no futurity but eternally is.

Hence the Word is in the beginning not in any temporal relation but in an eternal identity. It is not that the Word was in the beginning, and is now no more; or even that it still is in the beginning. It is that the Word is the beginning — so that it is impossible to conceive of the one without the other. No sooner do we turn toward the beginning than we find the Word already there. Just so, we cannot seek the Son without finding the Father, nor seek the Father without finding the Son. The one is in the other. In Gregory of Nyssa's formulation: "The Son is in the Father as the beauty of the image resides in the archetypal form [while] the Father is in the Son as the archetypal beauty resides in the image." Less platonically stated, the Father manifests his glory: he reveals his name. Thus Jesus prays, "Father glorify thy name." In other words, the beginning reveals the Word that the Word may reveal the beginning. The Word is the mediator.

As for the Father, who is as a father to his son(s) and outside whom there is nothing — or rather for whom there is no outside — this *arche* or beginning is the one unknowable, nameless cause and origin. Everything he is he gives to his Son, who returns it to him. Therefore, the Son reveals the Father; he is who the Father is not — that is, he is the visibility of the invisible, the knowability of the unknowable. But this is not to say that the Son is the opposite of the Father. There is no dialectic here. Rather, the Son is the difference of the Father's sameness. He is that in the Father whereby the Father may know himself. So the Son is generated while the Father remains; he is life, while the Father is death; he has and knows everything while the Father, who has given all to the Son, has nothing, knows nothing, and is nothing. The Father's life is his Son, who is his generation and his begetting.

All of this is to say that the name of the Father is the Son and the name of the beginning is the Word. "The name of God and Father, which is essentially subsistent, is his Logos" (Maximus). By this name the Father reveals himself. This is the unuttered name "above every name" — the name of the Father — that the Father gave himself in his Son, his Word. This is the name that the Son, his Word, manifested and declared.

This theme of meditation on the name of the Father was dear to early Christianity, especially in its gnostic moods. In the

Gospel of Truth, attributed to the great Valentinus himself, we find entire paragraphs like the following devoted to it:

> Now the name of the Father is the Son. It is he who first gave a name to the one who came forth from him, who was himself, and he begot him as a Son. He gave him his name which belonged to him — his is the name, his is the Son. It is possible from him to be seen. But the name is invisible, because it alone is the mystery which comes to ears which are completely filled with it. For indeed the Father's name is not spoken, but it is apparent through the Son. . . .

2

"Name" is one way in which the Son reveals (and conceals) the Father in a mystery; "image" is another. St. John, however, does not use either of these, but simply states that the Word was *with* God in the beginning. Now the force of this "with" (*pros*) is "toward": the Son is *toward* the Father as the Father is *toward* the Son. Thus their relation is active. They are together, toward each other, actively, not passively. The Son is actively with the Father — and this active "toward-ing" is none other than being the Father, that is, God himself. Therefore, lest we presume that the difference is one of nature, St. John adds, not only that the Word "was God," but that "this (the same) was in the beginning with God." In other words, there was no "time" when the Son was not. That much is clear. Less clear is the implicit teaching regarding unity and identity.

The principle of identity, according to philosophical tradition, asserts the unity and particularity of a thing — that a thing is one, and is itself, and is not other than itself. Usually this takes the form $A = A$, that is: A is (equal to, the same as) A. Thus it seems to require two terms and yet, for anything to be the same as itself, only one thing or term is required, but this one term must be placed "in relation to" itself. It must become "other" to itself. Identity is thus something understood as being in relation to itself. This is the sense in which the Word is "with" God — the Word is with God as God is "with" himself. Here we may note Heidegger's comment on Plato's saying in the *Sophist* that of two things, for instance rest and motion, "each of the two, let us be sure, is another, while each is with respect to itself the same." Heidegger points out that *heauto* (the same) is in the dative case, signifying that "each, which is itself, has been returned upon itself." Identity, whereby each thing is itself, is thus a relation, a belonging together. In identity there is mediation, connection, synthesis. The *same*, writes St. John, was in the beginning *with* God.

Thus the highest identity is not simple but an ineffable synthesis of unity and distinction, sameness and difference. This is the metaphysical "good news" announced by the Incarnation. If the Word is God, then God is complex, and the apparently empty, tautological abstraction — the reification — of identity is revealed as full, living, and concrete. Indeed, the Incarnation proclaims that the divine identity, through whom all things were made, contains all things: *all things were made by him*. In the everyday world of ordinary space-time consciousness, things make their claims upon us by their differences, but in themselves, outside space-time, all things make their claim upon us by virtue of their identity, of their being the same with respect to themselves. There a stone, placed before itself, being the same with respect to itself, makes its claim upon us as stone — absolutely. Similarly, plant, tree, star, galaxy — all make their claims upon us insofar as they are self-identical and the same with respect to themselves. And God, the unknown, nameless *nihil per excellentiam*, placed before himself, makes his claim on us as the Word — God, the All, the knowable Son. This is to say that even nothing placed before and with respect to itself is something, indeed is everything — identity as such, the I AM, the primordial ground of all. This is the tradition of St. John and

Eriugena: the cause, which is nothing, placed before itself, occasions its identity, which reveals, and hence contains in synthesis, the universe or all. "The absolute is concrete identity," writes Hegel in his *Encyclopedia*, "that is, an identity of and through all the differences of which it is the identity." It is this identity of which St. John speaks when he invokes the Word in the beginning, the same with God, God with God, together.

3

Our theme is identity and identity is "individual" — or rather it goes beyond individuality. Indeed, identity requires the sacrifice of individuality, the sacrifice of that which, separating us from the whole, makes absolute identity or true unity impossible. True identity is "emptied," open to visionary possession. A person cannot be whole and at the same time be cut off from, and opposed to, another. Inevitably, then, identity demands the idea of love, for love is the unconditional gift of significance to another. This is a supernatural act that depends upon both the continuous sacrifice of one's own individuality or egotism and the simultaneous discovery of significance for oneself. This sacrifice of self — whose paradigm is marriage — reflects the divine self-sacrifice and unity upon which all identity and creation rest.

In divine self-sacrifice, God distinguishes himself from himself, empties himself into himself, receives himself from himself. In order to be God with God, God becomes God, sacrificing himself to himself. Severing — distinguishing — his unspeakable oneness in an act of total, universal sacrifice and love, God sees himself in himself and, seeing himself, sees the universe. Thus it has always been. In the words of Pherekydes, "Zeus, about to create, turned himself into love." God gives himself to his Word as in a mirror so that, in the words of Oscar

Milosz, "His beauty, appearing freely and as though from outside, Love should be exalted above the law."

Such sacrifice, which is the substance of identity, is properly only divine. Only God can truly sacrifice himself for only he has a self to sacrifice. Hence all identity is in and of God, for outside God all sacrifice is the illusory projection of a fallen suffering.

Sacrifice makes sacred. To make the universe, his image and likeness, a sacred thing, God had first to make himself sacred. He had to separate himself from himself. Thereby he became who he already was and his identity, his original face, pre-existent until then, was revealed. Thereby, too, in the warmth and perfume of his sacrifice, in that movement of otherness, the sameness of life, love, and light are present. Thus St. Paul writes of "the odor of a sweet smell, a sacrifice acceptable, well-pleasing to God," and exhorts the Ephesians to be "followers of God, as dear children; and walk in love, as Christ also hath loved us, and hath given himself for an offering and a sacrifice to God for a sweet smelling savor." Through the savor — the odor of the sweet smell of sacrifice — sacrificer, sacrifice, and the receiver of the sacrifice are united in a single identity. Identity, truly, is the seed and fruit of sacrifice, love overflowing into love. As Solovyov writes, "When we say that the Absolute principle is by definition the union of self and its negation we are only repeating in a more abstract form the words of the great Apostle, God is love." God is love: he sacrifices himself to himself and the sweet savor of the universe — of love and the Holy Spirit — arises.

4

The Word is God's presence to himself, his identity in his interpenetration of himself. Therefore the Word says, "I am in the Father and the Father in me," not implying that they are interchangeable but suggesting a reciprocal, mediating relation whereby the one co-inheres in the other. Thus, "If ye had known me, ye would have known my father also." This is what the Word means when he says, "I am the way, the truth and the life; no man cometh to the Father but by me." Yet this is only possible because we, too, are in the Word and the Word is in us.

This is the sacrificial work of the Incarnation: "That they all may be one; as thou, Father, art in me, and I in thee, that they may also be one in us: that the world may believe that thou hast sent me. And the glory which thou gavest me I have given them; that they may be one, even as we are one: I in them, and thou in me, that they may be made perfect in one; and that the world may know that thou hast sent me, and hast loved them, as thou hast loved me."

The Father so loved that he sacrificed himself to himself and begot thereby his Word in whom the world, still spiritual, was made. All remained a single spiritual identity in and through the Word — who was that identity. But the world fell. But the Father so loved the world that he sacrificed himself anew in time, giving his Word or identity for the world he so loved. And as his self-sacrifice outside time gave Word and God identity in the beginning, so his self-sacrifice in time gave God and world identity in time through the Word. Human beings *are* the world and thereby we are called to participate in the free, self-sacrificial identity, the fundamental "with," "together," and "toward" of Father, Son and Holy Spirit, wherein each is at once distinct and the same.

5

The mystery of identity is also the mystery of creation. *All things were made through him* who was identity — God with God — in the beginning. With the sacrificial act of the Father's begetting of his Son — his uttering of his Word — all things were made in and through his Word. Here we step on hazardous ground for it seems that the begetting of the Word is itself creation. Yet, of course, they are different. This, for Eriugena, is the ineffable, foundational paradox, that "through him who was not made but begotten, all things were made but not begotten."

In the *Periphyseon*, Eriugena makes a fourfold division of everything that is and is not: "The first is the division into what creates and is not created; the second into what is created and creates; the third into what is created and does not create; and the forth into what neither creates nor is created." These four — God (1), the Primordial Causes (2), the universe generated in time and space (3), and the Return (*Apocatastasis*) of all things into God (4) — forming two pair of opposites, one created and one uncreated, account for everything, from the beginning to the end.

Creation begins with the "Primordial Causes," also called Predestinations, Wills, and Beginnings (*Archai*) of things. These are the archetypes or paradigms which the Father makes in the Word and divides into effects through the Holy Spirit. At once many and one, these *logoi* participate directly in the Trinity, without the intermediary of any creature. That is to say, they mediate between the divine unity and created multiplicity as creation unfolds. In a sense, they are God's ideas, but for Eriugena they are not identical with him because they are created. They are neither begotten like the Word, nor proceeding like the Holy Spirit: they are made. As for their number or order, which one would expect of created things, they have none. Like the divine itself, the Causes in themselves are one, simple and unseparated — separation or distinction only occurring in their effects, their phenomalization as theophanies in and to the contemplative mind.

Two premises underlie this anomaly. First, there is the fundamental distinction between Creator and creation, Uncreated and created. As Eriugena puts it: "The first and greatest division of universal nature is into the founded universe and the nature created in that founded universe itself." The second premise is the corollary of the first. Namely, "All things proceed from a single first principle." It follows that the first creatures — made things — proceed from the first principle, in the first principle, by the first principle. Eriugena writes of them: "They were made eternally, at once and together, by the Father in his in-born Word — i.e. his Wisdom — so that just as the Father's Wisdom itself is eternal and co-eternal with its Father, so all things made in it are eternal; except that all things have been *made* in it, whereas it itself was begotten, not made, and is the *Maker*." All things in their Causes are eternal in the Word, but not co-eternal. They are the same in their eternity, but different in their being made, not begotten.

Eriugena asserts, in addition, that God is free of accidents, meaning that creation cannot be accidental to him and that there cannot have been a "time" when he was not Creator. In other words: "He did not subsist before he created the universe. Otherwise the creation of things would be accidental to him." Yet, as Creator, causally, logically, God precedes his creation. As single First Cause he must be prior in some way. How? In the sense of containing his creation, as cause contains effect. Indeed, in this Neoplatonic tradition, "participants in a cause subsist in that cause." Hence, as Eriugena says: "If God precedes the universe founded by him simply in the sense of being its Cause ... and if God is not accidentally causal, but always is, was, and will be a Cause, and participants in a cause subsist in their cause — then the universe is eternal in its Cause since it participates in it." Therefore: "The universe of all creation is eternal in the Word of God."

What, then, is the difference between the universe in the Word and the universe we see and inhabit? For Eriugena what is important is "not that there are some things which are in God and learned to be in God because of the unity of nature, and other things which come into the world by generation; but that one and the same nature of things is observed one way in the eternity of God's Word and in another way in the established temporality of the world." God is called one because he is in all things universally. God is God — he only appears different depending upon our point of view, our state of consciousness. Ultimately, there is only God and therefore "all things in God's Word are not only eternal, but are actually the very Word of God itself." The implications here are staggering: all things were made in and through the Word, but what was made was not other than the Word, which was not made but begotten. Miracle of Miracles! The Word, through whom all things are made, is made in all things. The uncreated is created. Nothing is something.

6

Consider another approach. The Son is begotten of the substance, that is, the difference, not the sameness or essence, of the Father — for in essence the Father and the Son are one. They differ only in being Father and Son. The Son, the Word, is thus begotten of the Fatherhood of the Father, of the Beginningness of the Beginning. All things are created from God's "othering (fathering)" of himself, his "seeing (son-ning)" all that he wished to see. Now, for the Father to "wish" is to "see" — to will is to perform. God's willing and making are one and simultaneous. Where, then, is the line between created and uncreated? As Eriugena writes, "Either God's will is separated from God and joined to creation, so that God is one thing and his willing is another — i.e., God is the maker and his will is made; or, if reason forbids such a statement, God and his willing and everything he has made are one and the same thing." From this it follows that, not only are the primordial Causes created, but also that God — who is uncreated and forever transcendent — creates himself and that this creation is not just archetypal or spiritual but *runs through* the whole of creation. God, as Eriugena defines him, is, indeed, "he who runs through." He "proceeds into all things and is made in everything . . . contains all things . . . and is the creative Cause of everything, and is created and made in everything which he creates, and contains everything in which he is created and made."

At the exposition of these ideas in the *Periphyseon*, the student in the dialogue is amazed and paralyzed in thought. But the teacher chides him, disturbed that he would seek "reason in which lacks all reason, or understanding in what surpasses understanding." Then he concludes:

> How and according to what principle God's Word is made in everything made in him eludes our mental insight. Nor is that strange, since in sensible things no one can say how the incorporeal force of the seed, bursting out into visible species and forms, into various colors and fragrant odors, becomes manifest to the senses and is made in things, although it does not stop being hidden while it becomes manifest. And whether manifest or hidden, it is never deserted by its natural powers. Wholly present in all things, whole in itself, it neither increases when it seems to be multiplied, nor is diminished when it is thought to be contracted into a small number; but it remains unchangeably the same in its nature. For example, *it is no smaller in a single grain of wheat than in abundant harvests of the same grain; and, what is more remarkable, it is no larger in a single whole grain than in part of the same grain.*

7

All things, then, are at once eternal and made; and their eternity does not precede their making, nor their making their eternity. For their eternity is created and their creation is eternal in the dispensation of the Word which makes all and is made in all. There is thus a twofold creation, one in divine knowledge and eternity, and the other in time, but God is entire in each. There is only one world. Indeed, as Eriugena stresses, "We should not regard them as different but as one and the same." In other words, this world is in heaven now. It is not the case that "part of the universe subsists as eternal in God's Word and that part, outside of the Word, is made in time."

These are deep issues, liable to misinterpretation, and Eriugena has often been censured by Church Councils and critics as heterodox, a pantheist, and a follow of Origen. Origen, it is said, failed to distinguish between ontological and cosmological dimensions. In his thinking, as Florovksy puts it, "the logical link between the generation of the Son and the existence of the world was not yet broken." That is, Origen did not understand the Biblical notion of the radical contingency of creation. He was too Greek, for in Gilson's words, "It is quite true that a Creator is an eminently Christian God, but a God whose very existence is to be a creator is not a Christian God at all."

Such criticism, however, as Gilson himself confesses, is not applicable to Eriugena because it fails to consider his understanding of the creator-creation relation in the light of his doctrine of theophany. For Eriugena, *creation is theophany.* It is revelation, illumination; and the Creator is utterly transcendent, "above being," never to be found, unknown and unknowable. And yet he creates and, creating, reveals himself, i.e. creates himself. Creation is revelation, revelation is creation. "All that is revealed is light," affirms St. Paul. All that is, is light, echoes Eriugena. All things — human nature, the universe, each one of us — are divine lights, luminous theophanies. The universe, the human soul, is a vast light-filled discourse, every word of which is uttered in and by the Word.

Each word and thing, therefore, is and is not the Word. It is not the Word but reveals the Word and participates in the Word. As Gilson so justly maintains, everything that Eriugena writes should be read in the light of this precision, such that "when he says, for instance, that God is in all things whatever they are, or that God is the entity of all things, we should never forget that to him God is in each thing as the sun is in each and every light. But [he continues] even this is not quite true for, whereas both the sun and its radiance are light, God himself is in being as what is beyond being." In other words, it is the primacy of transcendence that saves Eriugena from pantheism and ensures the Creator his freedom and the "contingency" of his creation. Beyond being, the Creator is unconditioned, absolute, unknown. As Eriugena says, "Even the most blessed, in the beatific vision, will not be able to see the innermost secret of divinity." Not so strangely, therefore, while some have accused Eriugena of pantheism, others have held him to be guilty of separating God and creation completely. The key to this paradox lies in the mystery of human nature as the primordial theophany or creation. For Eriugena, human nature is at once the seed and fruit of creation, God's means of knowing himself. But human nature fell — and herewith a digression is necessary.

8

If all things were made by the Word, all things should bear his mark or trace and, looking about, we should be able to recognize his signature on every side. Should we do so, however, very likely what we will see first is something very different — some variant of sin, suffering, and death. Seeking to discover the trace of the Word in creation, we uncover the question of evil. True, the world clearly bears the traces of the Word's goodness, truth, and beauty, but it also and equally is deformed and girt about with suffering. Nor, apparently, is this suffering limited to the "human" world: it seems to consume the worlds of nature also. Indeed, from this perspective, an examination of the mineral, vegetable, and animal kingdoms reveals no paradisal state but rather a universal drama of "sickness unto death." Such, at any rate, is the Christian view. Good and evil, God and Satan rule together in a mixed, chaotic universe. If, therefore, the Word made all things, then either he had sin and death too, or they are unmade, or they do not exist.

The traditional account is simple. God is one, and any kind of dualism is anathema; he is good as such and by his nature cannot make evil because he is good; in fact, he cannot even know it, because for him to know is to cause to be. Sin and evil, therefore, having no cause, do not exist. Yet clearly they are very real for this world, since it was to overcome them and their Prince of Darkness that the Word incarnated. Theology stumbles at this point. Evil is said to be due to the abuse of the freedom with which God endowed his creation — or rather, which was his creation. But this freedom was given — made — by God, who is omniscient. Must it therefore be determined by him? If so, the drama of creation and the fall thereby turns into a game that God plays with himself. This is an idea which, as Berdyaev says, it is impossible to conceive of rationally. For who could understand that God "foresaw the evil and suffering of the world ... the perdition and everlasting torments of many," and yet created the world. Here, according to Berdyaev, is the "profound moral reason for atheism," for, failing all other answers, "the logical conclusion is that God has predetermined from all eternity some to eternal salvation and some to eternal damnation. . . ."

It was precisely this Augustinian doctrine of double predestination that Eriugena was called upon to combat in his controversy with the monk Gottschalk. For Eriugena, since God is one and good, there could only be a single predestination — to Godhood. Yet to speak in this way is improper, for God is independent of time while predestination depends upon it. Nor is there any necessity in God. His will is free and humanity, made in his image, is likewise free. God "permits" human activity. When this activity moves toward the good, he knows it; when it moves towards what is not good he does not, because for him it does not exist. Its existence does not derive from him. And yet it "exists" in some sense; we experience it as suffering;

and so it must have a cause of some kind because there is "nothing visible or corporeal which does not signify the invisible or incorporeal."

Therefore, in his *Commentary*, speaking of John the Baptist's saying, "Behold the Lamb of God that taketh away the sins of the world," Eriugena writes:

> The sin of the world is original sin, which is common to the whole world, that is, to human nature in its entirety. . . . Original sin is this: all human nature, in which all human beings from the beginning to the end are one, which was created at once and together in the image of God, and created body and soul simultaneously — this human nature, unwilling to observe God's commandment, transgressed the divine laws in paradise by disobedience.

The cause of suffering, then, is a spiritual act — disobedience — in which human nature *as a single organism* participates and which precedes the coming-into-existence of the visible world we presently inhabit. This means that, as Eriugena is careful to point out, "The first Adam, he who of all human beings came before all others into this world is not the first to have sinned, for all have sinned before entering this world." Adam, as an "individual" is not to blame — indeed, there is no such being. Adam, rather, is "human nature in its generality . . . born by way of generation into this corruptible world" — which would not have happened if "the offense of human nature" had not come first. We are all "in" Adam, as we are all in the Word. "This general sin is called 'original'," Eriugena concludes, "since it is the common origin of all."

But the common origin that the world and all things in it share is paradise or original human nature, nature as such. This origin is the creation of all things in the Word. But somehow this paradise, human nature in its natural state, transgresses, disobeys, giving rise to the world we know and inhabit. This transgression is also original and common. Committed by the whole, the whole bears its mark of suffering and death. This is to say that, though all things were made in the Word — and nothing was made without him — nothing is as he made it.

This is why in gnostic and Neoplatonic teaching the soul herself has a negative aspect, suggestive of a falling away or defection from a more spiritual condition. Plotinus, for instance, in the celebrated opening of his *Fifth Ennead*, writes:

> What can it be that has brought souls to forget the Father, God, and, though members of the divine and entirely of that world, to ignore at once themselves and it? The evil that has overtaken them has its source in willfulness [*tolma*, also "boldness," "rashness"], in the entry into the process of becoming [*genesis*], and in the primal differentiation and the will to belong to themselves. Rejoicing in their freedom [*autexousion* or "self-determination"], once they had come forth, they made ample use of moving on their own, taking the contrary road, and defecting to such extremes of distance that they lost the knowledge of their origin in the divine.

The will to self-determination and self-ownership are for Plotinus the motives of the souls's defection and fall into becoming. But did the world of becoming pre-exist to receive the soul — human nature — in its fall? Do suffering and evil pre-exist our experience of them? Plotinus, like Eriugena, makes it very clear that the world of becoming, with all its debts and burdens, is the fallen soul herself.

In *Ennead III, 7*, Plotinus, writing of time and eternity, asserts that in the primordial, paradisal unity there was no time, no becoming. How then did time come to be? Plotinus writes:

> As it were "before" — prior to having engendered this "before" and become needful of the "after" — it reposed in and with Being and was not yet time, but was itself at rest in that Being. But there was a nature which was forward, and wished to own and rule itself, and had chosen to strive for more than was present to it. Thus it started to move, and along with it also moved time, and movement was

toward the ever-still-coming and later toward the not-selfsame but ever-again-other — and once having travelled some distance of the way we have brought forth time as a copy of eternity. For there was in the soul an unquiet power, which always wished to transfer what it had beheld There into another medium, unwilling to let the present totality be present to her.

Thereby the soul temporalized herself, dividing herself into phases and parts, concealing her unity and wholeness. Beginning to move, she became time, because time is movement. Simultaneously, her thinking and consciousness — what she is — also became temporalized: i.e., discursive and comparative. As Plotinus so succinctly states:

Since the cosmos moves in the soul — for nothing other than the soul is the place of the sensible universe — it must also move in the time of the soul. As the soul imparts her activity in portions — one succeeding to another, and again succeeded by a different one — she generated succession as such along with her being active; and at one with discursive thought, which each time is different from the preceding one, each time there came forth in creation what had not been before. . . .

In other words, movement, which is time and discursive thought, quantized the soul and spatialized "matter," producing a second creation. For if movement is time, it is also space; and space is none other than the "materiality" of matter. Put another way, the soul, beginning to move, awakes in herself an infinite desire which, seeking fulfillment, hurls the soul into the indefinite quantification of unlimited space.

Hence there are two souls (and two matters), one in eternity and as it were unfallen, the other in space-time, fallen, and subject to multiplication and division (suffering) without end. In time, matter is without identity. Neither alive nor spiritual, it is but "a dead thing decorated." Ceaselessly changing its form, it is (in Plotinus' words) "a new entity in each separate case, so that nothing is permanent and one thing endlessly pushes another out of being." But in eternity "intelligible matter" is a living, spiritual existence. Immutably one and the same, it is all things at once and therefore it has nothing to change into: "it already and ever contains all." This unfallen matter is the pure potentiality of being, its seed-power. Called in unwritten Platonic teaching the "indefinite Dyad," it is the number Two, flowing forth from the One, unlimited in potential. Without extension, it is pure activity, a dynamism without movement. Flowing forth, it returns; returning, it is informed. Informed, it reveals the One to itself in a motionless motion Plotinus likens to vision: "a seeing which sees itself." Such is paradise, the original cosmic being, true human nature.

For unfallen, intelligible spiritual matter is primordial soul, a proclivity for seeing and contemplation, a potentiality for vision that awaits a sight. Therefore we may even call it "darkness," for sight is light. It is the darkness of deep potency, not a darkness of privation or lack — a virgin, primal, creative darkness, without memory, desire, or understanding. Filled with sight, however, impressed with her true object, this soul is love — "the love [as Plotinus says] which is an eye filled with its vision, a seeing that bears its image with it." Thus soul — human nature — in its true state is the living, qualitative medium of God's vision of himself.

In Christian terms: projecting himself, God sacrifices himself to himself. Thereby he knows himself. And because he is infinite, he projects himself infinitely and, constantly returning to himself, orders and measures — determines — his infinitude. What he measures is not "matter" as we know it; it is his own theophanic qualities, his Divine Names. Then — something happens! Rather than returning upon God as is her wont and obediently reflecting his infinite mercies, soul or matter turns from God, from paradise, and temporalizes herself in an urge to self-determination. Thus she falls, forfeiting her wholeness, and shamelessly revels in the illusory plenitude of phenomena.

Possessing everything by nature, but only insofar as God, bestowing it on her, draws it forth, the soul wills to possess something in her own name and nature, for herself. This is the gnostic story of the fall of Sophia. Her desire separates her; God and unity recede; suffering and fragmentation become her lot. She has lost her spouse, the Word. Only the Word, her spouse, can save her now. Shapelessness, eternal need, utter poverty become her world. "Evil" arises.

Thus human nature, a divine creation made for eternal contemplation of the divine, became exiled from her true country and became a principle of boundlessness and horror, a place of deepest darkness and ignorance. Here, created not by the Word but by the soul herself, are all the poor, illusory things of this fallen world — universal egotism, hatred, violence, falsity. Truly, as the Russian philosopher Solovyov wrote, "What lies at the basis of our world is being in a state of disintegration, being dismembered into parts and moments that exclude each other." Indeed, with the fall into time all things became separated by a twofold impenetrability in which each moment of time excludes and exists at the expense of the next and two bodies in space become tragically unable to occupy the same location. Worse still, there is an impenetrability to knowing as well as to things known, and the principle of temporalization produces not only the sufferings of physical impenetrability or false existence but also those of "cognitive impenetrability" or false knowing. Here we have the temptation of knowing one thing at a time, to which the temptation of Adam and Eve refers.

From this point of view, the lapse is from a single, unified knowledge (which is, by definition, knowledge of the Good) into a situation in which the essence of a thing and its appearance are split apart, so that thought can no longer seamlessly and timelessly unite concept and percept, but is forced to struggle with endless dualities of form and matter, inner and outer. The fruit of the forbidden tree is not evil, but a mixture — a false, duplicitous thing, the unpacking of which in time creates only confusion, relativism, and death. For life is to know all things whole, in the Word, and the Word, whole, in all things. But the serpent tempted Eve, the soul or *anima*, and she succumbed, surrendering to her senses, and the sensible universe began its evolution; then Adam, who, following this analogy, we may call spirit (mind) or *animus*, fell also — without a moment's hesitation, as befits a timeless gesture — and thereby the sensible universe became conscious and death "hurt."

In this way all creation, made invisibly in human nature in and by the Word, unfolded as from a seed into conscious sense-perception. Objectified time and space gradually became the arena of suffering. And though indeed all things were made by the Word in the Word — and nothing was made without him — now things began to evolve on their own, with a created *karma*, a destiny, memory, and desire of their own. For though this *karma* has its origin and continuation in the mysterious faculty of freedom, which is the uncreated gift of the Highest and perhaps is human nature itself, this *karma* took on the burden of a life in time that was not its own. Indeed, this perhaps is the greatest sacrifice: that the divine in all things fell and assumed the fallen condition as its own. And if this is the case, then it is the divine in us and all things that suffers being torn apart in a mixed world of good and evil, joy and pain, truth and error. No wonder that God, the freedom of the uncreated, to ensure the *apocatastasis* or final restoration of all things, had to save his fallen freedom by enacting his sacrifice — giving his *life* — in time.

9

Therefore St. John proclaims, *What was made in him was life*.

Eriugena proposes two ways to meditate this. Either: All things made in him were life — i.e., what was made was life in him. Or: What was made in him — i.e., what he is — is life. In both cases the life referred to is necessarily "eternal," but whereas in the first case it is a created eternity, a divine grant of immortality which is our created nature, in the second case it is clearly the Holy Spirit itself that is in question — which is not a made eternity but eternal reality itself, the divine presence embracing and pervading all. If the Holy Spirit is life, then life truly is an "eternal and perfect power," the transcendent principle of reality's unveiling. "Spirit is living and life is spirit," wrote Paracelsus, for whom "the special life of each thing is a spiritual being." For him, the form may be destroyed, but the spirit — the life — is indestructible, spirit and life being for him "essentially one, not two." But are they? And if not, who will tell the dancer from the dance? For all things dance and, dancing, mirror the endless, co-inhering round-dance of the Trinity. Therefore, to understand the life made in the Word, we must always bear in mind that this life, like all else that is essential, is an ineffable circumincession of made and unmade, of holy life and un-created spirit.

Divine nature — Reality — is unknowable, and yet, as Eriugena writes in the *Periphyseon*:

> Theologians have correctly deduced from the things that are that it *is*, and from their division into essence, genera, and species, differences and individuals, that it is *wise*, and from the stable motion and moving rest of things, that it *lives*. In this way they also discovered the great truth that the Cause of all things is of a threefold substance. For, as we have said, from the essence of things that are it is understood to *be*; from the marvelous order of things it is shown to be *wise*; and from their motion it is found to *live*. Therefore the cause and creative nature of all things is, and is wise, and lives. And from this those that search out the truth have handed down that in its *Essence* is understood the *Father*, in its *Wisdom* is understood the *Son*, and in its life is understood the *Holy Ghost*.

St. Maximus, too, speaks of God himself as "unknown Mind, unuttered Word, and incomprehensible Life," and calls the Holy Spirit "the consubstantial Life of the Father," just as he calls the Son his "consubstantial Wisdom."

The Father knows his Word on his Breath, for his Word lives on his Breath. Indeed, his Breath is the life of his Word in which he himself is and is wise. Together Word and Breath manifest the Father. Thus the perfect, inseparable bond of Word and Spirit is made evident: the Word cannot be uttered if the Breath does not proceed. Similarly, in Plato's *Sophist*, the Stranger points out that reality cannot stand "immutable, in solemn aloofness devoid of intelligence," but must be intelligent, which it cannot be if it does not possess life, and neither intelligence nor life, he claims, are possible without "the soul in which they reside." Plotinus, too, proposes a threefold nature to primal reality which likewise is, and knows, and lives. Though the order of his three often changes, Plotinus is consistent in assigning life to procession — "a power of ever-fresh infinity, a principle unfailing, inexhaustible, brimming over with its own vitality." Determined, this principle of life is Wisdom; undetermined, it is Being. And though Plotinus will sometimes organize these three hierarchically, there is no question that for him the Three are One — "a unity co-extensive with all, as our universe is a unity embracing all the visible" — and that Life is authentically primary.

Life, thus, is motionless movement, procession: a unifying unity and a creative power. Following Porphyry, later Neoplatonists, employing Aristotelian terminology, will speak of being, life, and wisdom — the abiding, the proceeding, and the returning — as essence, power, and activity, a triad fully Christianized by Eriugena's mentor St. Maximus, who introduces the idea of "will" in place of "power" or "life." Since God can only act what he wills, what he wills he must accomplish: his power of accomplishment is identical with his will. This power of will — life as divine will — St. Maximus then distinguishes according to two modes which he calls Providence and discrimination. Providence is "that which maintains the cohesion of the whole," while discrimination has to do with "the maintenance of the difference between things ... which safeguards to each creature its connection with the *logos* after which it was conceived." Here life is "the inviolability of individuality" or suchness. This is the traditional, ancient teaching in which the cosmos is "one mass of life," its soul — "a divine source of unending and rational life for all time" — regulating and unifying its manifest multiplicity into perfect order and harmony.

But what *is* this life? Clues abound. Chief among these is that Life is Love — as the life of the Holy Trinity is love. For the Father sacrifices himself to himself, gives himself totally to himself in a movement of self-sacrifice and self-emptying, thereby becoming the bridge between himself and himself. This bridge of love, holding apart and binding together, is without direction. There is neither time nor space where it flows. Simultaneous and reflexive, it is "the joy of the Father and the Son from before all ages." Above all, it is *affirmation* — a great Yes! — a fountain of joy forever. The Father affirms the Son, the Son affirms the Father, their love interpenetrating in total, divine-cosmic affirmation. Denying themselves, they affirm each other, their separate "no's" becoming a common "yes." Truly, the life which is love is a great and endless Yes!

It is to this tradition that Swedenborg refers when he writes, "No one can know what the life of man is, unless he is aware that it is love. . . . *Love is the life of man.*" Some idea of this love, Swedenborg continues, may be formed from a consideration, according to the doctrine of correspondences, of the heat of the sun in the world. Swedenborg writes, "The Lord, being love in its very essence, that is, Divine Love, appears to the angels in the heaven as a sun, and out of that sun proceed heat and light. The heat proceeding is love, and the light in its essence is wisdom." Thus love and heat mutually correspond to each other; and life, which is love, is warmth. This view is not unique to Swedenborg. Rudolf Steiner also states, "No man can know what warmth is who is not able to form a conception of what it means to be ready to sacrifice what he has, everything he possesses, indeed, not only everything he possesses, but also what he himself is." Such a sacrifice, as the Father's and the Son's, Steiner continues, must be *free*. It cannot be constrained at any level, but must be essentially open, without outer compulsion or motive. Pure, sacrificial love must arise out of a fully determined inner determination to give what one is, one's life, wholly to and for another. Whoever would find his life must lose it. From such acts an "inner warmth of bliss" arises and the universe is made sacred and alive. Such is the glow of sacrifice which is eternal life and which lies at the foundation of all that is and is not. For just as in the Godhead the bridge of sacrificial love is without direction, so life in the universe is equally present. It cannot truly be said that one thing has more life than another. Likewise love, when it is in deed and truth, shines on all without distinction, just as God himself "maketh his sun to rise on the evil and the good, and sendeth rain on the just and on the unjust." Therefore St. John teaches us to love one another without distinction. As the Word loved us, we must love one another; as he emptied himself of his divinity and sacrificed himself for us, we must empty ourselves in sacrifice for each other — for that is what it means to participate in the life made in him.

This life-giving, self-emptying death and resurrection is called *agape*, which is eternal life, the gift of the Holy Spirit. It is participation in the Lamb slain before the foundation of the world, and slain again in time on Golgotha. By the slaying, at once the Father's self-slaying for the Son and the Son's self-slaying for the Father, the world is founded and is full of life. All things made in him were life because they pulsed with the living light-and-life blood of the Father and the Son. Love is the essence of life in the laying down of life. Therefore the good shepherd gives his life for his sheep, and therefore we should all be shepherds, giving each other our lives for the sake of the whole. This is why Jesus says, "This is my commandment, that ye love one another as I have loved you." Greater love hath no man than that he lay down his life . . . but he must do so freely, there must be no compulsion, for if the laying-down is not free what should be an act of ego-transformation will become an act of egotism, and the love will not be holy, but neurotic and distorted. It is for this reason that Jesus says, "No man taketh it from me, but I lay it down of myself. I have power to lay it down and I have power to take it up again. This commandment I have received of my Father."

"Commandment," here means not so much injunction as "pattern" — the example to be followed. Thereby the life which is love becomes the mystery of reciprocation. As Jesus, who is reciprocation, says, "The Son can do nothing of himself, but what he seeth the Father do; for whatsoever things he doeth, these also doeth the Son likewise. For the Father loveth the Son, and sheweth him all the things which he himself doeth." Thus the sacrifice, which is life, also shows and reveals. It is knowledge and identity: our original face. Truly loving, we open ourselves utterly, disclosing and receiving all that we are. This revealing-receiving identity gives, and is, love and life.

By this life, which is sacrifice and love, all things are in the Word and are life. In space and time, things only have a semblance of life. They suffer, die, and pass away. In themselves they are nothing, but in the Word they are eternal, their suffering and passing has meaning and value. In the mutual sacrifice of Father and Son, in the holy place of their love's circulation, things truly are.

10

In the beginning, in the Word, *God created*. Creation or "creativity" is the link between God and his Word and his Word and us. Thereby divine sacrifice — love and life — the ineffable bridge between unmade and made, is revealed to be creativity itself: the ability to begin, to create out of nothing. In this ability all things are held in their potentiality. For what Boehme calls "the fountain of joy in the whole of the Father" is none other than the seed of the universe, of which the gnostic Basilides wrote that it "contained in itself the whole seed mixture of the world." Within this seed, in single perfected potency or gesture, lives the life-power, essence, and identity of all things. In itself, this life-within-life is unknowable, because we are it — or rather, it is us — and yet, since all things, including ourselves, participate in it, we may know it by thinking into its effects.

From this point of view, nothing is dead or lifeless. Forms may be annihilated and disappear, but life itself is an eternal power. Therefore Eriugena counsels us to recognize the eternal life in all living things. Particularly, of course, he asks us to consider the power of *seeds*, how, as we have quoted before, "the incorporeal power of the seed, bursting out into visible forms and species, into various colors and odors, becomes manifest to the senses and is made in things, although it does not stop being hidden while it becomes manifest." More than that, this life-power is continuously and everywhere *whole* — "no smaller in a single grain of wheat than in abundant harvests of the same grain." And yet each seed is specified, each thing under the sun having its own seed — its particular suchness — which makes it what it is and none other. The Seed of seeds, then, the Word, contains the specificities of all particular things, just as each particular seed contains its own appropriate specification.

Contemplating the mystery of the seed, we find each simple thing of nature unfolding as from an invisible spiritual essence, which is its synthesis and virtuality, through germination, stalk and leaf, to close upon itself in seed-containing fruit. This closure of seed with seed implies that to describe the process as "unfolding" is not quite accurate. Considered in its wholeness, the seed in its various metamorphoses seems rather to be a single, timeless reality that only appears spread out in time but is in fact one and single. This is the vicious circle of the seed, and circular thinking generally, wherein one's thinking must continually rise from effects to cause and descend from cause to effects — a circle which, as Koyre says, "the mind cannot understand, but which life resolves as it plays itself out." Life certainly seems to resolve it in time, but if we are to follow Eriugena's injunction and, beginning with visible things, trace all things back by a kind of spiritual hermeneutics to their true life in the Word, then we must strive to overcome time, or at least withdraw from it and leave it aside. To do so, to move out of the passing-time of the physical world, is to begin the process of restoring things to their origin. It is to begin to reconnect beginning and end, birth and death, and so, in some degree, it is to heal the universe and to heal ourselves.

But what is it, finally, that is lead back in this process? As Henry Corbin has shown in numerous studies, it is none other than the soul itself that is led back and returned to itself. This is to say that, as the visible world reveals itself in this Word-like way to a Word-devoted consciousness, the soul awakens to its own true living nature. For the soul, according to this tradition, is one with the universe viewed symbolically: it is the universe of symbols. Soul and world are one. And symbols — for such a symbolizing consciousness — are synonymous with seeds. Out of them grows the universe.

To realize this is to live in the Word as Imagination, in the sense in which Blake called Jesus the Imagination. In himself, the Word, the divine Imagination, contains all things in dynamic, living synthesis. Thus Blake wrote, "To the eyes of the man of Imagination, Nature is Imagination itself," for life — *natura naturata* — is the imaginative power working in nature and mind alike. In other words, not only is life "the internal copula of things," as Coleridge called it, it is also the common ground where divine and human, God and world, meet. It is even, in this sense, God's own ground and unity. All beams from his life; all dwells and is contained in him. He is the living place at the center of all things, the sun of sacrifice from which all things radiate, by whom they grow and develop. Such is the Word's seminal power of life and imagination in this spherical, sensible world of light and life which we inhabit — this world which is life and light.

11

In his little treatise, *On Light, or the Beginning of Forms*, Robert Grosseteste, Bishop of Lincoln and Head of the Franciscan School at Oxford, Eriugena's disciple in this manner of thinking, writes of the universe coming into being as light. Light, he writes, is volume and body. By its very nature it diffuses and multiplies itself in every direction so that a point of light instantaneously produces a sphere of light of any size whatsoever. This spherical universe we inhabit is such a universe of light, luminous in essence, living in creativity. Therefore Eriugena says *omnia quae sunt, lux sunt*, all things that are, are light; which is the same as saying, *omnia quae sunt, vita sunt*, all things that are, are life.

12

To understand all this we must understand something of the relationship between thinking and being as Eriugena outlines it in the Fourth Book of the *Periphyseon*.

He begins by asserting the basic premise of his anthropology, namely, that "humankind was produced from the earth in one and the same genus with the other animals; and that beyond the nature of all animals it was made in God's image and likeness." He does not, however, propose that human beings are in any way dualized or possessed of two souls; nor does he suggest, as Plotinus does, that there is a part of the soul that is unfallen — indeed, if the humanity were not wholly fallen, it would not have required Christ's deed to raise it up. This is not to say, however, that the soul — the whole human being — cannot live outside "time" and "matter" and "in" the Word, but only, paradoxically, that if a human being does so, he or she does so as a whole. It may be useful to speak of body, soul, and spirit, but this is not to divide the indivisible person. The soul as a whole is present throughout. As a whole it is life, intellect, reason, memory, and as a whole it is at the same time "outside all creation and itself (for it is included among the number of creatures)," revolving about the Creator in intelligible and eternal motion when purged of all vices and images. In other words, not only does the soul occupy several places at once, it is also simultaneously in and out of place, in and out of time — but whole in every place. Such is our mysterious nature that we may be as a whole present everywhere in the whole — discoursing with God and his angels in heaven, while endowing with life and growth, perception and thinking, on earth.

It follows that the human being is in a special way co-extensive with the universe. As Eriugena notes, "Wise men agree that in human beings universal creation is contained. Human beings understand and reason like angels; they have sensation and govern their bodies like animals; and hence all creation is understood to be in them." Corporeal, vital, sensitive, rational, intellectual — such is the division of creation, all of whose aspects are contained in humanity in every respect. More than that, just as God is both above everything and in everything, whole outside everything and whole in everything, so human nature also is "whole in itself, in its universe, in its visible and invisible parts; whole in its whole and whole in its parts." At the same time it exceeds its whole, for if it did not how could it know its Creator? Eriugena explains: "A person who clings to him is above all things and above himself." In other words, we are fallen and unfallen; and, indeed, though fallen, it is our unfallen nature which is our true nature. As Eriugena writes, "We should not judge human nature by what appears to the senses. . . . Everything that God created in it primordially remains whole and intact, but it is still in hiding while it awaits the revelation of the sons of God."

What, then, is our world, the world of human nature, wherein human nature is everywhere whole, and whose light the Word is? Eriugena is unhesitating. Human nature is creation, creation is human nature. There is no other. In human nature creation is brought forth; through human nature creation will be returned and restored. That is why all of creation groaned and travailed in pain until now.

The mystery we must fathom is that of human nature in its world. When Eriugena turns to this question his argument is based upon the traditional teaching that what understands is prior to what is understood, that the idea of a thing is prior to that thing itself. That is to say that knowledge of things in divine wisdom — the Word — is prior to the things of which it is the knowledge. Indeed, from this point of view, the substance of things is the idea of them in the divine mind. Nor is human nature exempt from this law: "A human being is a certain intellectual idea eternally made in the divine mind."

Human nature likewise, in its knowing, precedes what it knows, containing it as idea. Therefore for Eriugena the Book of Genesis, by giving Adam "dominion" over nature and bringing all creatures before him to be named, clearly indicates that primordial human nature contains the "ideas" of all the things of nature brought before it. In other words: human nature contains perfect knowledge of creation. Furthermore, just as God's uncreated knowledge is the uncreated substance of creation, so human or created knowledge is the created substance of what it knows. For the substance of a thing is to be found where it is understood; and this is true even of a human being's self-knowledge for, as Eriugena says, "the very idea by which one knows oneself is believed to be one's substance." But did we not say that the substance of a human being is the idea of him in God? There is no contradiction. A human being, like everything else, is one thing in itself and another thing in God. What a human being is rests in God; that a human being is depends upon that human being's understanding.

Putting this together we arrive at the startling conclusion that there is a point of view from which *"we may appropriately say not that humanity was produced from the earth in the genus of animals, but rather that the genus of animals was produced in humanity from the earth."* Humanity here is human nature, created consciousness, wherein all things were made. We are used to this idea in the case, for instance, of geometrical figures. When two people think the idea of a triangle, they both "perceive" the same idea: there are not as many triangles as people thinking them, but a single idea of a triangle that all contemplate. It does not surprise us therefore that the true substance of a triangle should reside in an intelligible reality accessible to human consciousness. But we are not so accustomed to considering natural objects in the same way. And yet, why not? As Eriugena says, "Why is it remarkable, then, if natural bodies too, compounded from the qualities of cosmic elements, subsist in that nature in which knowledge of them is present...?"

Human nature thus is a second god, a god made in the image of God, for an image is at once similar to and different from that of which it is the image. The difference, of course, is the difference between uncreated and created, but beyond this absolute abyss "everything else predicated of God can be predicated also of his image, but predicated of God essentially, and of his image by participation." In other words: "If human nature had not sinned and had clung without change to him who created it, it would certainly be omnipotent." Eriugena therefore writes:

> As the creative Wisdom, God's Word saw all things that we
> made in it before they were made, and the vision itself of
> the things seen before they were made is their true,
> changeless and eternal essence; so created wisdom, which
> is human nature, knew all things in it before they were
> made; and the knowledge itself of the things known before
> they were made is their true, abiding essence.

Created wisdom, then, the knowledge which is human nature,
is "the second essence and effect of higher knowledge." This is
true with regard to all things. For creation proceeds "from the
knowledge of the creative wisdom through created wisdom."
Through human nature all things were made.

Thus human nature is a direct reflection or effect of divine
nature. All things are in the Word causally, and are life, and this
life effectively is the light that lights human nature: its effect is
the light of human nature, that human nature reflects and is
illuminated by. This light is not human nature, but human
nature bears witness to it and is illuminated by it. Human nature
is that witness. In other words, for Eriugena, human nature is a
receptacle or mirror whose beginning and end is to reflect the
light of life, without the interposition of any element foreign to
it. This is our source, from this we derive, towards it we
journey.

But what is the path, how can such divine self-knowledge
begin? Where does it begin? In the *Periphyseon*, responding to
the question of when a human being receives knowledge of his
nature, at his "first" creation in the primordial causes before the
"times of the world" or at "procreation" upon entry into time,
Eriugena replies, "In the one generally and latently; but in the
other specifically and openly in the effects." This is because, he
then confesses, it is only in the effects — in time — that
individuated knowledge can count as specifically *human* self-
knowledge. In the primordial creation of human nature there is
only a single, universal, divine knowledge. There all human
beings are one — one divine-cosmic human being containing all

humanity. Human nature there is an undivided, undifferenti-
ated, unconscious unity and, as such, it cannot have knowledge
of itself. Only by entering this world, only by distinction and
differentiation of that nature into the *things* of this world, is
such knowledge possible.

Yet human nature is always one, indivisible, and seamless.
And nevertheless it appears in two ways — as two forms of
divine presence: life and light. Understood in and by God, we
are life; understood in ourselves, by ourselves, we are light. And
light, in this case, is but a particular aspect of life. "If there is to
be light, there must be fire" (Boehme). Light reveals the fire of
life; the fire manifests itself as light. As Boehme says, "When love
becomes revealed in light by means of fire, it streams over
nature and penetrates her, like sunshine penetrating an herb or
fire penetrating through iron."

All things are made life in the Word; in human nature and
the cosmos they are made light. But human nature and the
cosmos are in the Word and in the Word they are life. Light is
life there. Indeed, between these two, as Eriugena repeatedly
says — between the mind (light) which knows the truth and
the mind (life) which is the truth — no creature is interposed.

Again, then, we return to the question of the relation
between the intellect and the Word. For Eriugena these two are
always two aspects of a single reality — but exactly how baffles
all understanding. They are two, but one; one, but two; wholly
one and wholly two, just as the Word himself, through the
Incarnation, is wholly human and wholly divine and wholly one:
"one substance in two natures." His humanity and his divinity
are inseparable, yet each of his natures is "unimpaired." Eriugena
calls this unity of divinity and humanity in the Word Christ's
"inmost, secret marriage . . . prepared before the creation of the
world." What is this secret marriage? Eriugena explains as best
he can:

> The Word united to the flesh and the flesh united to the
> Word in an inseparable unity of one and the same

substance from two natures, divine and human, receives only those who gaze at the unity of its substance with the simple eye of perfect contemplation. As a human nature in the Word is truly the Son of God and the Word in human nature is truly the Son of Man without any transformation of natures, Our Lord Jesus Christ is understood as one and the same Son of God and Son of Man.

The reunion of light and life, truly divine and human, will only occur when, through the return of the world into human nature, human nature, the light, is restored to the source of life, which is the Word. This is the *apocatastasis*, the restoration of all things at the end of time. It is the return of the second creation into the first, a mystery at once metaphysical, cosmological and historical, at once future, present, and past, in time and out of time. On all levels the Word, the light of human nature, is active — for the Word was made flesh. To participate in the Word, in his life, is to assent to this incarnation and have "eternal life." Eternal life is then the light of human nature. Human beings fell away from that life; and the light fell into the dark abyss of cosmic time, unfolding the universe as we know it. Thus the light is scattered in the darkness and in need of recollection.

13

Darkness, like nature, has two faces. What we may call original darkness is life and light in the Word. The second darkness is "fallen" and does not know the Word which is life. It is ignorance and death. Refusing life, it does not know light. The original darkness, on the other hand, is the Word-bearer, the divine reflection and vessel of the true light. It is this darkness which is "the light of men."

Turned in self-will from the divine light, this darkness — which is the light of men — turns sour. Its truth becomes error, its obedience becomes disobedience. Hatred, greed, envy, pride — the works of this second, fallen darkness are well known. What is not recognized is that they are the works of darkness, demonic creations that darken the inner eye, rendering it blind to the true light and the true darkness.

This fallen but originally true darkness is the darkness of the "flesh" which, from this point of view, is the central Christian mystery. Here, for instance, is how St. John Damascene invokes the flesh in his work *On Images*:

> Together with my King, my God and Father, I worship him who clothed himself in the royal purple of my flesh, not as a garment which passes away, or as if the Lord Incarnate constituted a fourth Person of the Trinity — God forbid! — The flesh assumed by him is made divine and endures after his assumption. Fleshly nature was not lost when it became part of the Godhead, but just as the Word made flesh remained the Word, so the flesh that became the Word remained flesh, being united to the Person of the Word.

Therefore, he continues: "I do not worship matter; I worship the Creator of matter who became matter for my sake, who willed to take his abode in matter; who worked out my salvation through matter. Never will I cease honoring the matter which wrought my salvation! I honor it, but not a God. How could God be born out of things which have no existence?"

Form, flesh, matter, human nature: these are one darkness. Nothing in itself, this one thing is given highest respect and greatest dignity — is illumined, redeemed, even deified — by its assumption by the Word. This is the meaning of the Incarnation. Yet even this cannot be quite correct. For if it is nothing, this darkness could neither fall nor be redeemed and deified; and if it is something, that "something" must be divine already, since from this point of view only God is. Therefore Eriugena calls it "darkness" because it lacks distinction. Having no distinction, it can receive and reflect the fullness of the light and its distinctions. This is the first darkness. The second darkness is the darkness of our self-willed, self-feeling distinctions that distort and obstruct the light rather than reflect it. The first, on the other hand, is a purely potential, divine receptacle. Thus, echoing Genesis, Eriugena writes of human nature that "investigated and considered in itself," it is found to be "without form and dark." Therefore we may think of it as one with the earth. And we may recall that "darkness was upon the face of the deep," and that "the Spirit of God moved upon the face of the waters. And God said, Let there be light: and there was light." In the words of Eriugena: "Human nature is not naturally light, but only participates in the light."

Invoking Genesis in this context proposes the idea that the Incarnation and its consequences constitute a second creation — or at least a reflection or repetition of creation. Here we cannot be too careful, for precisely with regard to creation Eriugena's thinking is most subtle and complex.

For Eriugena, to ask what creation is, is to ask what humanity is, and to ask what both are, is to inquire after God — the question that includes all questions. Cosmology, anthropology, theology are thus aspects of a single quest. This is to say, finally, that for Eriugena creation is none other than God's creation or revelation of himself. God appears to himself: that is the miracle of creation, that is why there is something rather than nothing. God in himself is unknowable, even to himself; in himself he is divine darkness; but he condescends to his creation, to making himself known to himself, in himself, to his creatures, by means of his creatures — his effects or actualizations, which we may call, with Eriugena, his "theophanies." By these he bursts forth from divine ignorance and darkness into divine knowledge and light. These two — God and his theophanies — are not two, but aspects of one. Indeed, as Eriugena writes: "We should not understand God and the creature as two things removed from one another, but as one and the same thing. For the creature subsists in God, and God is created in the creature in a wonderful and ineffable way."

Returning to Genesis, we find that "in the beginning God created heaven and earth." According to Eriugena, this means that in the Word the Father made the primordial causes of all things invisibly and immaterially. Since the causes are still wholly turned towards the Word and have not yet proceeded into their effects or manifestations, the "earth" is described as "without form, and void." That is: without space, time, mass or anything that might determine physical form, the earth is empty of effect or distinction. And where is human nature here? For Eriugena, this is human nature. Constituted of heaven and earth, linking and joining these in a single unity, human nature is none other than the totality of the primordial causes. But who or what is this "first" Adam, made up of the primordial causes of all things? Since it cannot be the Word itself, it must be the first theophany — the theophany of theophanies. Such is human nature's origin and destiny — to be first created thing, the theophany of the Trinity, the archetype of all creation.

Here especially we must remember that no created nature ever possesses anything but what it has been given. For the creature, being itself is a gift. To be is to receive being, as to live is to be given life. This is fraught with implications for, as the tradition says, all gifts have their source in the Father, their archetype in the Son or Word, their distribution in the Holy Spirit. These must do their work. It cannot therefore be completely proper to describe the totality of primordial causes as if they were already completed human nature. Rather it should be said that they are the potentiality of human nature, whose full realization requires the entire process of creation, incarnation and resurrection — from the Word in the beginning to the Word made flesh to the restoration of all things.

PART THREE: THE WORLD
(*Homily*: Chapters XIV-XXIII)

1

What the world was for the Greeks, history was for the Hebrews. The Greek *cosmos* was the language of God uttered in space, which is static and abstract, while the sacred history of the Hebrews was that same speech uttered in time, which is concrete and dynamic. In the Greek cosmos each natural thing in space was a hieroglyph situating a moment of creation and so was a mode of access to the living worlds of form and archetype. The Hebrews, for their part, saw each natural or historical event as prophesying the end of time and so situating a temporal moment of return. The Greek view of time was cyclical; salvation was individual and out of time; knowledge was a permanently available spiritual state. For the Hebrews, on the other hand, history or time was itself salvation; salvation was collective, and knowledge was an evolving spiritual state.

With the Incarnation these two views of the world, Jewish and Greek, interpenetrated and were reconciled; though perhaps only we today, Jews and Greeks in the twentieth century, can realize it. For the Word who incarnated — died, resurrected, and ascended — was both the Greek principle of cosmic harmony and the Hebrew principle of History. He was the "Alpha and Omega" of the one, and the Logos or Word of the other. Naturally, neither Jews nor Greeks could accept this, for the Cross which was the medium of their meeting was too terrible and shocking a device, as St. Paul well knew when he wrote, "For the Jews require a sign, and the Greeks seek after wisdom; but we preach Christ crucified, unto the Jews a stumbling-block, and unto the Greeks foolishness; but unto them which are called, both Jews and Greeks, Christ the power of God, and the wisdom of God. . . ."

The Word, then, the self-communication of the divine in time and history, connotes the entrance into the world of both the Greek *Logos* and of its Hebrew counterpart, which is perhaps best termed "Righteousness." The Word is wisdom and righteousness: by his Incarnation he unites cosmos and history, redeeming and sanctifying both in a single deed. But this event, shameful and incredible as it appeared (and indeed still appears) was neither a simple prophecy such as the Jews could understand nor a metaphysics such as the Greeks could appreciate. Neither could understand it. And yet the events recounted in the New testament are both of these — prophecy and wisdom — but in so absolute and nondualized a manner that neither Greeks nor Jews were ready for it. For the Greeks still inhabited a two-level universe in which the phenomenal, historical world was not the archetypal world of order but only dimly echoed it as a shadow does its reality; while the Hebrews lived in a world in which the world to come — the real world — was not the world they lived in. The Word changed all this. With one sudden, gratuitous eruption into time, heaven and earth, this world and the next, were made one. This is to say that with the Incarnation the heavenly world, the world to come, invaded and permeated the earthly world. "Before the Incarnation of the Word of God," wrote St. Gregory Palamas, "the Kingdom of Heaven was as far as the sky is from the earth; but when the Kingdom of Heaven came to dwell among us, when he was pleased to unite himself with us, then the Kingdom of Heaven came close to all of us."

No longer was there any unbridgeable gap between here and there, present and future. The Greeks had sought after wisdom, but now that wisdom had come in person, in St. Paul's words, "Christ, in whom are hid all the treasures of wisdom and knowledge ... the wisdom of God in a mystery, even the hidden wisdom, which God ordained from before the world unto our glory." And this Greek wisdom was the same as that which the Hebrews had sought in "signs" in the realm of historical time. For the Jews waited for the "fullness" of time and watched for signs of it in God's timing — in the righteousness and timeliness with which he appropriated to every purpose and each thing its proper time. It is to this that the Word refers when he says, "My time has not yet come, but your time is always ready," and, being crucified, cries out, "It is finished" — that is, time is *fulfilled* according to its measures. Just so, St. Paul wrote, "When the fullness of time was come, God sent forth his Son. . . ." And again:

> Blessed be the god and Father of our Lord Jesus Christ, who has blessed us all with spiritual blessings in heavenly places in Christ: according as he hath chosen us in him *before the foundation of the world*, that we should be holy and without blame before him in love; having *predestinated us unto the adoption* of children by Jesus Christ to himself, according to the good pleasure of his will ... wherein he hath abounded toward us in all *wisdom* and *prudence*; having made known to us the mystery of his will, according to the good pleasure which he hath purposed in himself; that *in the dispensation of the fullness of times* he might gather together in one all things in Christ, *both which are in heaven and which are on earth* ...

The references to being chosen before the foundation of the world, to being predestinated to adoption, imply a history of salvation *from the beginning*. The divine plan, never deviated from by an iota, was that God should be all in all. The human-worldly fact of the fall, freely occurring, changed nothing. History became part of the process; God's self-communication became historical, his sacrifice temporal. Thereby the history of the world became the history of salvation — salvation offered to human beings as revelation. Indeed these three — revelation, salvation, history — are but different names given to what we may call "human existence." History, therefore, is but another name for the universal body of humanity. Through this body human beings experience, act and suffer their destinies on the field of their freedom and reflection. But with the resurrection history is over: it has been fulfilled.

This is the key: time is no more, we have become time. The prophetic foreshadowing has given way to reality itself. With the Incarnation, human beings dwell in realized time. The Kingdom has come. Now grace and truth abound. The Law, time itself, has been fulfilled, raised up and transformed. We are part of a new creation: the creation in time. We can begin: out of nothing, in freedom, in and with the Word, we can create in time as the Word created in the beginning.

2

Therefore, as the Gospel says, "In those days came John the Baptist, preaching in the wilderness of Judea, and saying, Repent ye: for the kingdom of heaven is at hand." Ascetic, his raiment made of camel's hair, a leather girdle about his loins, his meat locusts and honey, this John must have been a terrifying figure. For the mercy of his baptism and the compassion of his confession of sins were more than balanced by the rigor of his demand for "fruits meet for repentance" and his denial of all that was not individual effort and intentional suffering. The individual — naked, solitary, existential — was his single focus. He demanded that each stand authentically, responsibly on his own ground. But people are stubborn and set in their ways, so that the Baptist had to cajole and threaten them, saying, "Think not to say to yourselves, We have Abraham to our father; for I say unto you, that God is able of these stones to raise up children unto Abraham. And now also the axe is laid to the root of the trees: therefore every tree which bringeth not forth good fruit is hewn down, and cast into the fire. . . ."

This Baptist was the *forerunner*. He knew that the Word

who came after him in the flesh came before in reality. He knew
that he baptized with water for repentance or "change of heart,"
while he who was to come after him — the latchet of whose
shoes he was not worthy to unloose — would baptize with the
Holy Spirit and with fire. The Baptist knew this from his
mother's womb, for in his mother's womb he had already
recognized his maker and leapt for joy. Despite this, the
mightiest came before the least. The Baptist could not understand this; he remonstrated; but Jesus overrode his objections,
saying, "Suffer it to be so now; for thus it becometh us to fulfill
all righteousness." The hour had come to reveal the Triune God
and to mark the transformation of Adamic humanity in the
Word. So Jesus went to be baptized, the heavens opened, and
the Holy Spirit descended like a dove, and the Father spoke:
"This is my beloved Son in whom I am well pleased."

There are four moments in the life of Jesus through which
the Incarnation of the Word unfolds: his birth, his baptism, his
transfiguration, and his resurrection. These four moments,
though each in a sense contains the others so that they may be
distinguished but not divided, mark the transformation of the
world. In this process, the baptism is the beginning of the
Word's ministry. Two of the Evangelists indeed begin their
story at that point and say nothing of the birth. Here we
approach matters fraught with controversy, for according to a
very old tradition it was not until the baptism that the Word
— the divine *Logos* — actually incarnated in the chosen and
perfect human being, Jesus. Thus the apocryphal Gospel of the
Ebionites — early Jewish Christians under the leadership of St.
James, the brother of Jesus — states that the voice of the Father
from heaven affirmed not only "Thou art my beloved Son, in
thou I am well pleased" but also *"This day I have begotten thee."*
Upon this basis the Ebionites believed, as did (and do) many
gnostic Christians that it is the baptism which marks the descent
of the Word.

It is important not to be dogmatic or reductionist. One

view is not to be pitted against another, as if God's truth could not contain more reasons than we may at any moment rationally comprehend. The situation is more complex, as Clement of Alexandria suggests when he writes, "Let us ask the wise, Is Christ, begotten today, already perfect, or — what were most monstrous — imperfect? And if imperfect, is there some addition he requires to make? But for him to make any addition to his knowledge is absurd, since he is God. For none can be superior to the Word, or the teacher of the only Teacher. Will they not then own, though reluctant, that the perfect Word, born of the perfect Father, was begotten in perfection, according to economic foreordination. . . ?" In other words, the perfect becomes more perfect. The baptism did not add anything, yet it added everything. It was a moment in the single Moment of moments. Therefore the Orthodox Liturgy proclaims: "Thou hast filled us with wonder at thy strange birth from a Virgin in ways past nature, O Word of God, and now thou dost exalt in a glory, a great mystery: by thy holy participation in the waters of baptism, thou makest the font rich in children through the Holy Spirit. The earth has been sanctified, O Word, by thy holy birth, and the heavens with the stars declare thy glory; and now the nature of the waters is blessed by thy baptism in the flesh, and mankind has been restored to its former nobility." This is to say that there are stages to the Incarnation as there are stages to any process occurring in time. Before the Word, the great Sun, could shine forth on the banks of the Jordan, driving out sin and darkness and illuminating the universe, he had to rise from a Virgin as from a cloud — or so it is said. And who shall say in any process where one stage begins and another ends. Certain things become clearer at certain moments, that is all. The baptism reveals the absolute divinity in Jesus: he is the Word, not just the chosen Son of the Living God, but God the Word born of God before all times. The baptism reveals the Trinity more clearly than any other moment — of this there is no doubt. The Father speaks, the Spirit descends, the Word is revealed. Therefore John introduces John into his theology. The Baptist is the precursor of the Theologian, for both recognized in Jesus the uncreated Word.

Indeed, the Baptist was the first to recognize the Word as Word and in that recognition the world was judged and created anew. In his *Commentary*, Eriugena quotes an interesting interpretation of the relationship between the forerunner and the Word that he attributes to St. Maximus. Eriugena writes:

> John is the figure of repentance, because he preaches repentance; Christ, on the other hand, is the figure of justice, not only because he judges the world, but because he himself is eternal justice. It is usual, however, only to repent after one has transgressed justice. This is to say that human nature, which transgressed the divine laws in Paradise, preaches and practices repentance in the person of John, and openly proclaims in him that the justice of the Word is preferred before him according to divinity, but comes after him according to the mission in the flesh. This is so that human nature, leading a life conformed to those divine laws that it scorned in a gesture of pride, should be recalled to its original state of justice.

John the Baptist thus speaks for the idea of *conscience* — indeed, he is the *voice* of conscience, as the Word is conscience itself. And yet it seems that the purpose of the repentance preached and represented by the Baptist is a return to a paradisal, pre-lapsarian state — an intention that accords well with his strategy of withdrawing from the world. This, indeed, is one aspect of what made him the last of his kind, a boundary phenomenon. He stood at the end of a long, noble tradition of seeking to return to some pristine original condition. But it was precisely in this that the incarnation of the Word introduced something radically new, something that shattered the old preconceptions just as it rent the veil of the temple. For the eruption of the divine into time and human nature meant that now, instead of seeking a paradise that was lost, humanity was called upon to build up out of its own nature a new "paradise." Therewith — with conscience — spiritual progress became evolutionary and embodied in time rather than seeking to escape from it.

As voice, the forerunner proclaims the new creation. The waters of the Jordan in which he baptizes renew the primordial waters, the waters of the first creation. In the beginning, only original nature was given by the waters, but with the baptism and the incarnation grace comes also by the waters of the Holy Spirit. John, however, only baptized with corporeal water and in the geographical Jordan, but since then, in the words of St. Gregory of Nyssa, "The river of grace runs everywhere. It does not rise in Palestine to end in the neighboring sea, but it envelops the entire world and plunges into Paradise, flowing against the course of the four rivers that flow from thence and carrying back into Paradise things far more precious than those which came out. For these rivers brought sweet perfumes and the cultivation and semination of the earth; but this river brings back human beings born of the Holy Spirit. . . ."

These beings born of the Holy Spirit are those who have repented and been baptized, for the forerunner preached repentance and the imminence of the Kingdom of Heaven, baptizing in Jordan and confessing sins. In this sense the forerunner, as the voice of conscience, in the inner solitude — the wilderness — of his own being proclaimed the possibility of *metanoia*, of the transformation of the heart which is the preparation, the vessel or organ for the Kingdom whose coming he foretold. He taught that *metanoia* and confession opened one to the Kingdom, to the presence of the creative Word in the beginning. In other words, he stood at the brink of the renewed human ability to say, Not I, but the Word in me.

The idea of confession and its corollary "sin" is a difficult one. In order to begin to understand it we may note that sin is in many ways a transformation of a prior and more "primitive" perception of evil which Paul Ricoeur calls "defilement." In this primordial meaning, evil is something quasimaterial. It is "out there" and it infects and harms not so much by any evil consciously committed as by a simple, objective violation of a law or tabu. Once such a law is violated, retribution, impersonal and cosmic, follows, inflicting pain, suffering and loss. These are the wages of defilement and at this stage there is still an absolute connection between the violation of a cosmic law and human suffering in the cosmos. There is not yet any separation between physical and moral spheres: they are one. As Ricoeur says, "Ethics is mingled with the physics of suffering, while suffering is surcharged with ethical meanings."

With the story of Job, this unity begins to break down, preparing the ground for a spiritual, rather than a physical, understanding of evil. The medium of this transformation is the human relationship to God and, following Job, personal piety begins to replace ritual purity as the true end of human life. For Jahweh establishes a personal covenant between himself and his people; and thereby sin becomes a personal matter between a person and his God. What was once the violation of a law, now becomes the violation of a personal relationship: a betrayal, a rupture, a revolt. Sin becomes at once the abandoning of God and the abandonment by him — the being cast adrift in nothingness or absence of meaning. Thereby a choice was laid down: God or nothingness or — amounting to the same thing — God or idolatry. For the idolater, making his fabricated divinity an object in itself rather than an "image" or "window," becomes cut off, immured by his projection, and cast into nothingness. "All the gods of the nations are nothing," proclaims Psalm 96. When the Baptist calls for repentance, then, he calls people to turn *away* from things and *toward* the spirit. "By returning and being at rest, ye shall be saved," says Isaiah.

Thus through the development of the idea of sin unfolds a consciousness of *personal* responsibility. As "fault" becomes ontologically "sin" rather than "defilement," it is experienced subjectively as guilt, and with guilt the possibility of *conscience* arises — indeed the possibility of guilt already implies responsibility and responsibility, in turn, implies conscience. At the same time sin, as a falling away from God, is accompanied by an ever-increasing development of self-consciousness. Self-consciousness and conscience arise together in relation to a personal God. Each human being now finds himself or herself placed in an indissoluble one-on-one relation to God — who is ever-present, ever-watchful, ever-ready to be pleased or angered. Responsibility, conscience, the interiorization of self-consciousness follow, becoming, as it were, "the God within," God's witness or recorder in the human soul. Therefore the Psalmist cries out:

> O Lord, thou hast searched me, and known me. Thou knowest my downsitting and mine uprising, thou understandest my thought afar off. Thou compassest my path and my lying down, and art acquainted with all my ways. For there is not a word in my tongue, but, lo, O Lord, thou knowest it altogether.

God sees all that human beings do and thereby human self-observation — the examination of conscience — becomes necessary. To examine one's conscience indeed becomes the imitation of God — the attempt to know oneself as God knows one. In the Old Testament, this knowledge is only proposed as an ideal; it is not yet attainable in practice because true examination of conscience can still be carried out only by God. Thus the Psalmist cries out, "Search me, O God, and know my heart: try me, and know my thoughts: And see if there be any wicked way in me, and lead me in the way everlasting."

The problem is that if God finds wickedness, the responsibility is mine alone. The context may be collective — we are all human beings — but the responsibility is by definition individual. Hence there arose the concept of the Torah or "Law." Because each person is individually responsible, a subtle understanding of what God expects in every case had to be worked out. The aim was to help people do God's will, but the result made the law a curse. A mass of legalisms, a complex system of merits and demerits arose. Hypocrisy and self-righteousness inevitably affected those who "knew" the law, while the rest fell victims to a suffocating sense of guilt and inadequacy. St. Paul returns repeatedly to this double danger inherent in the law — for he knew by experience that one cannot by definition satisfy the law, for its commandments are in principle unlimited, as God is, while human beings are finite, limited creatures. Thereby fulfillment of the law becomes impossible. Indeed, more than that, it seems "the law entered in that sin might abound," for "cursed is everyone that continueth not in all the things which are written in the book of the law. . . ."

Into this complex situation the forerunner erupts, calling for the abandonment of all pretension, above all, paradoxically, the pretension to be autonomous and self-constituted. The evolution of consciousness among the Hebrew people had culminated in an explicit, rational understanding of responsibility — which, in turn, gave rise to a powerful sense of self-consciousness. Now the forerunner mercilessly called for the abandonment of this I, demanding its reversion, its emptying and sacrifice, its return to God. Such is the repentance he calls for or rather predicts — for he is not yet himself that return but only stands for the possibility of it. This is why he is called "the friend of the bridegroom." Auguring something new, he is not yet what he augurs. Though "among those that are born of woman there hath not arisen a greater," "he that is least in the kingdom of heaven is greater than he." For the least in the kingdom of heaven is born not of flesh and blood but of the spirit. Self-consciousness and autonomy are the height of flesh and blood's aspiration, but rebirth in the spirit is consciousness and autonomy of another order.

The Baptist represents something very great: the highest human nature can attain in its humanity, in its I. But now this I must stand aside, it is not high enough. Human nature must rise

higher still. The kingdom of heaven draws near, divinization by
the Holy Spirit, by fire, approaches. The baptism of John, which
is by water, insofar as it serves to remind one of the pre-
lapsarian state, prepares for this, but it is not the thing itself, for
that is newness as such. John as Elias — the Baptist in his
previous incarnation as Elijah: "And if ye will receive it, this is
Elias who was for to come" — was precisely the prophet who
above all others spurred on the ascent of self-consciousness
while the God of the chosen people gradually emerged as the
single One and demanded from Israel, his people, unwavering
devotion and obedience. In his contest with the prophets of
Baal, who stood for the differentiated worship of multiple
powers, Elias/Elijah demonstrated the overwhelming power and
superiority of the Single One, the great and only I AM — not the
wind, or the earthquake, or the fire, for these could still be
confused with the gods of Baal, but the ineffable, transcendent
I AM, heard "in a still small voice." By the acknowledgment of
this Other, the human, interiorized counterpart of the still small
voice, the "here I stand" grew stronger.

Elijah and John the Baptist are two aspects of a single
process. For the emergence of the idea of a continuing individuality, immortal in its passage through the cycles of birth and
death, is the mirror image of the single, immaterial, immortal
deity. The forerunner, from this point of view, represents the
culminating human experience of the personal God that Juda-
ism proposed. Elijah and the Baptist stand here for the whole
Jewish tradition and represent, as such, a rocklike self before a
rocklike God. Again and again Elijah, humbly proud, says to his
Lord, "Here I stand." I.I.I. . . . But St. Paul will say, ushering in the
new dispensation, "Not I, but the Christ in me." This the great
reversal. The permanent witness, the true individuality is called
upon to unite with, to lay itself down before, the spiritual
witness, the Word from the beginning.

Truly, this new thing requires a radical turning upside
down and inside-out of all existing values. This is what it means

to live at the turning of the times: "Behold, I make all things new," said the Word. Until the forerunner, creation unfolded, materialized, individuated. With the baptism, with the Word's incarnation, spiritualization begins. God unfolded the world into individuated human beings; now these human beings are called to fold back that world into God. Thus the forerunner stands at the edge of an abyss separating two infinite moments — an abyss called "Jordan" in the Bible. On the banks of the Jordan, in Bethany beyond Jordan, John baptized. "Bethany," as Eriugena tells us, means "House of Obedience," and there are two of them: one on this side of the river, where John baptized, the other, near Jerusalem, the heavenly city, where the Word raised Lazarus, who is said by some to be no other than the Beloved Disciple, John the Theologian himself. The baptism and the raising of Lazarus thus stand in polarity as the end of the old and the beginning of the new. John, by his baptism, made the people aware of their divine origin. But that was all he could do. He could not bring them closer to it. The incarnation changed all that. Grace abounded, and the dignity of the beginning became the real hope of the end.

3

Above all, however, the Baptist is the witness: the first called upon to testify in the supreme trial upon whose issue the fate of the whole world hung. Indeed, from a juridical point of view, the entire New Testament is a cosmic legal document, the defense's final testimony and the summation of its case. Thus the four Evangelists testify as to what they have seen and heard as "eye-witnesses and ministers of the Word." And St. Paul too testifies, as do the writers of the Epistles and the Book of Revelation. Finally, of course, the Word's own presence, his incarnation, may also be seen as the paradigm of testimony — as the legitimation of divine, cosmic, human and historical witness.

For the Son bears witness of the Father, as the Father bears witness of the Son; and the Paraclete, the Comforter, bears witness of the Father and the Son, as they do of him.

But among human beings it is the Baptist who is singled out — indeed, is sent — to be a witness and so an example of witnessing. As an Old Testament prophet, the Baptist is the last of his lineage: he must give way to the new witness, the "Not I, but the Christ in me." Preparing for this, in the fullness of his I, he shows the way, he stands on the edge. Having seen and heard, known and believed, he proclaims and interprets what he has witnessed. Truly, his is an eyewitness account. Having seen, he affirmed in an unconditional affirmation what he had seen. But he did not do so rationally or dialectically. He did not present logical proofs — for such is not the role of the witness. The witness must rise above a personal perspective. He must empty himself, become simply eye and ear and, appropriating what he has seen and heard, give expression to it without any interposition. The witness is only called upon to know. His experience must be certain — dialectical reasoning can have no place in it. This is to say that testimony and witness speak from and to the *heart* — so that false witness cannot be reduced to an error in things seen but must rather spring from the heart of the witness who saw. False testimony results from a bad heart. The true witness is the faithful one whose heart is always open.

There is thus something unconditional — divine — in witnessing. If witnessing connotes such absolute, heart-open, faithful affirmation, then what is affirmed and witnessed can only be attained, in the final analysis, through the divine. Witnessing thereby becomes the identification of what is divine in us with what is divine in the world. The witness must "put off the old man, which is corrupt according to the deceitful lusts." He or she must be renewed, must put on "the new man," the Word. To be a true witness calls for renunciation — above all the renunciation of the cerebral mind, that vain presumption to be self-constituted and master of one's world — a world in which the heart is only a physiological pump and not an organ of perception and knowledge. Renouncing all possessions, the witness — the true martyr — follows the hardest of the Word's saying, namely, "Sell all that thou hast, and give to the poor, and follow me." The witness possesses nothing. As the Baptist says, a human being has and is nothing unless he receive it from heaven.

4

Specifically, the Baptist bears witness of the light that is the meaning of all things and the light of the world, the true light which lightens every human being entering the world. For this reason the Liturgy calls him "the candlestick of the light," the ray of the sun, the friend of the enlightener. This light he calls the "Lamb of God." In his *Commentary*, Eriugena writes:

> When John says, "Behold the Lamb of God," he reveals him openly to the people. The Word of God is called "Lamb" by him because it was the Word who under the law was prefigured by the mystical lamb. Nor should we be surprised if the shadow predicates the truth. The shadow is the lamb of the law; the truth, so to speak, the body that casts the shadow, is Jesus Christ. Nor is he unreasonably called the Lamb, for the lamb furnishes three things to those who possess him: milk, wool, and his flesh to eat. Our Lord does the same. He furnishes the clothing of virtue for those who believe in him; he nourishes them with milk, that is with the simple doctrine of the truth; and finally he leads them to the perfect food of divine contemplation. Christ is called the Lamb of God because he was sacrificed for the whole world. And that is why the Scripture adds, "which taketh away the sins of the world." He takes away sin not by transporting it from one place to another, or from one time to another, but he takes it away entirely, so that none exists. Through the destruction of his most

sacred flesh, he totally destroyed the sin of the world. This sin of the world is called "original" because it is common to the whole world, that is to say to all of human nature; its barb is removed by the grace of baptism, but sin itself will not be fully destroyed until the resurrection of all at the end of the world.

What is original sin whose barb the Lamb of God takes away? Eriguena continues:

Human nature in its entirety, created whole and at once in the image of God, in which all human beings from the beginning of the world to the end are one — for all human beings were created in it, body and soul — this human nature transgressed the divine laws in paradise because it was unwilling to obey the commandments of the Lord. In truth Adam, who of all human beings first entered into this visible world, did not sin alone, but all sinned before his coming into the world. For the words of the Apostle, "For as in Adam all die, even so in Christ shall all be made alive," should not be understood to refer only to the first human individual. The individual Adam would, in fact, not have been born by way of generation into this corruptible world had the offense of human nature not preceded him. For the division of nature into two sexes, male and female, and the generation thanks to which, beginning with those two sexes, the human species develops and grows in number, are the punishment for the general sin by which the whole human race, at one and the same time, transgressed the commandments of God in paradise. Thus this general sin is called "original" — and rightly so, since it is the sin of our common origin. Because of this sin all humanity, with the exception of the Redeemer, are subject to death and corruption. Indeed, of the whole mass of humanity, only the Redeemer remained without sin. Only by him who was the only human being ever untouched by sin could the wound of all nature be cared for and all wounded nature be brought back to the health of its original condition. Hence both original sin and all the individual sins contracted after generation are forgiven by our Savior in the abundance of baptismal grace, to the point that they no longer exist. This is the meaning of what the Evangelist writes when he says, "Behold the Lamb of God which taketh away the sins of the world." The Word is the mystical Lamb, the one and only. The lambs which the people of Israel sacrificed each year in spring, one for each household, prefigure him. As for us, who after his incarnation, passion, and resurrection believe in him and who, in the measure that grace is given unto us, apprehend his mysteries, we sacrifice him spiritually and eat him, not with our teeth but intellectually.

This Lamb of God, whose blood takes away the sins of the world, is the same Lamb slain from the foundation of the world. As Eriugena writes in one of his poems, "If you wish to understand the Passover, first study nature" — that is, how "the structure of the world is said to be abundantly translated from nothing into particular species, how the Creator brought forth the causes which in bright forms clear with light he had always with him." Redemption is truly a second creation — a creation in time. In other words, bearing witness to the Lamb, the Baptist witnesses at once and simultaneously the sacrificial action of the Word in the creation of the world and his future sacrifice for the end of sin and the promise of the new creation: the *apocatastasis* or final restoration of all things in their suchness in God. The Baptist's knowledge was complete, but he did not (and could not) live to "see" the Lamb slain. Before that could happen, he had to die. Insofar as he was the forerunner, he came before, and could not receive the fruits of the Lamb. Therefore he is called the "friend" of the bridegroom, but not his "bride" — not "that great city, the Holy Jerusalem, descending out of heaven from God."

The Bride of the Lamb, prepared for by the Baptist, is in the widest sense the resurrected cosmos: the human, risen counterpart of Paradise. The Lamb, slain for the resurrecting of the cosmos, is the hook, the germ of fermentation, which will raise up the world. "Lamb-ness," in other words, is none other than "divine human-ness" — the complete, interpenetrated union of spirit and flesh. It is the principle of incarnation and the power of deification. It is to this light that the Baptist bears witness.

5

At the time of the Incarnation of the Word, the world lay shrouded in darkness. Following it, the world — though illuminated now by the Light — still labors in the delusion and obscurity of a sense-world apparently cut off from the light of true knowledge, the world of meaning. But this duality is now illusory, for the Light has shone, and the way to unity has been re-opened. The whole world seems to lie in wickedness, in sickness and sin — and yet it is saved. But that is not our experience; or it is not yet our experience. Today, indeed, many people do not even experience the duality of things, they do not recognize the fact that things are not as they should be. Yet it takes no special gift to realize that, as the Buddha taught, suffering is the first truth of human life and that, in the words of Solovyov, "Evil is a world-wide fact; all natural life begins in violence and wickedness, goes on in suffering and servitude, and ends in death and putrid dissolution."

To experience life from this perspective is to confront the absurdity, the meaninglessness of life. Nothing has meaning. Everything is absurd, cut off, disconnected from any relation or context that would give it meaning. This is to say that evil and absurdity (meaninglessness) are here the same and rest upon a demonic foundation of fragmentation and discord. But to see evil as the lack of meaning is to realize that meaning — unity, wholeness, harmony, connectedness — is possible. And because things do not fall apart completely — because evil does not utterly overwhelm the world — because things do cohere and even suggest qualities of meaning — truth, beauty, goodness — we may conclude with Solovyov that a unifying tendency must exist and be present, however dimly, as the true reality, forever guiding, sustaining, and drawing all things into relation with each other and itself.

The mystery here — which is the mystery of the new creation — is that this one true or real world of meaning seems to be "invisible" — a thing of the mind alone, ideal and fleeting. Certainly it is the world of virtue, grace, love — above all, love — and wisdom; and as such it seems for the present a shadowy thing, uncertain at best, impossible at worst. Certainly, it is not the world most of us see, for what we see is the world of egotism, selfishness, violence and death. But are these things the only visible reality? Or could the invisible world of gráce and love become visible and swallow up and remove without a trace what we presently see as a visible nightmare? Could we make the world invisible? Could we awake one day and find ourselves transported into the world of truth and light and realize with a relief bordering on disbelief that the world of darkness that we had endured so long was an illusion and gone forever? St. Paul writes, "We know in part, and we prophesy in part. But when that which is perfect is come, then that which is in part shall be done away with. . . . For now we see through a glass darkly; but then face to face; now I know in part, but then I shall know even as I am known." And St. John in his *Epistle* says, "It doth not yet appear what we shall be; but we know that when he shall appear, we shall be like him; for we shall see him as he is."

For Eriugena, at the end of this world all "will be dissolved and returned to its causes." For "all things which proceed from the Cause of all things and from the primordial causes established in it always strive by a natural motion for their beginning, outside of which they cannot rest." This is as it should be. Indeed, "all things flowing from the Source of all things would become worthless and utterly perish unless they were able to return to their Source and actually did return." Therefore:

> Our mortal bodies will be transformed not only into
> spiritual bodies but actually into our souls, because natural

necessity prescribes that just as a rational soul made in
God's image is to return to Him in whose image and
likeness it is, so the body too, made in the image of the soul
and, as it were, the image of the image, will, when freed
from all earthly weight and corporeality, be returned to its
cause, the soul; and through it, as a kind of mean, it will be
turned into the unique Cause of all things.

This, of course, is the restoration of humanity "to its pristine
state in him who assumed it wholly, namely in God's incarnate
Word."

The question of timing, however, remains awkward. In
general, the Fathers — among whom we may count Eriugena
— conflate the final return (*apocatastasis*) with the process of
its coming to pass (*theosis* or deification). The paradox of time
overwhelms them. What alone is clear is that the transformation
they speak of is real — as it was for the poet Rilke who wrote:

> It is important not only to run down and degrade all that is
> here, but also just because of its provisionalness which it
> shares with us, these phenomena and things should be
> understood and transformed by us in a most fervent sense.
> Transformed? Yes, for it is our task to imprint this provi-
> sional, perishable earth so deeply, so patiently and passion-
> ately in ourselves that its reality shall rise in us again
> "invisibly." *We are the bees of the invisible. Nous butinons
> éperdument le miel du visible, pour l'accumuler dans la
> grande ruche d'or de l'Invisible (Madly we gather the
> honey of the visible to pile it up in the great golden
> beehive of the Invisible).*

This is a real raising up of the sense-perceptible into the
spiritual. Sin, death, suffering — all the paraphernalia of the
prince of the world — are overcome. The world dwells in the
light. Suddenly the veil of phenomenal reality is punctuated and
permeated by God's transcendent Word, his presence.

And human beings are opened to the continuous restoration of the world. Is this not a miracle? Is not the world magic?

The Word which spoke from without now speaks within. A new age dawns. The knowledge of the continuous creation of the world always foresaw the *apocatastasis* of all things. Now, with the Incarnation of the Word, this possibility is seen and handled. This is what is meant by the saying that "all things are made new." No longer is the sensible world ignorant, dark, lonely, its denizens toiling under a single cosmic law of suffering; no longer need we feel abandoned and destitute in a material world of fragmentation and disunion. The world is raised up; clad in a glorious body, potentially at least it is now a body of glory, its materiality drenched in uncreated light.

For us, post-Incarnation human beings, this process has already begun. In that sense it is accomplished already. Indeed, we may say that it is both gradual and instantaneous: we both participate in it now and look forward to it. Watch and pray, teaches the Word, for you do not know when the great transformation will come. Unlike the physical sun, which rises dutifully every day, you never know when the spiritual Sun, rising, will shine suddenly into the darkness of your life.

6

Of the two worlds or natures — the old and the new, the false and the true — their falling apart, their relationship, and their coming together, St. Paul has much to say. He describes the one as sense-determined — as an inherited sense-body. Its characteristics are sin and death; and to live in it is to live in fear and to labor in bondage to the prince of this world — who is determinism and harsh necessity. He speaks of the other as a world of peace and blessing. This is the world of the "spiritual body," whose characteristics are grace, freedom, life, and hope. The first he calls the world of the old or earthly Adam; the second is that of the "new man," the second Adam who is the Word. In Adam all sinned; in the Word all are saved. From Adam up to the resurrection of the Word, humanity lived under the old covenant of the law; but after the resurrection the world lies under a new covenant, which is the gift of grace. The new covenant, however, is not just a correction of the old: it is brand new, a new creation. With the coming of the new Adam and the divine permeation and raising up of the creature through his incarnation, death and resurrection, the great reversal began. A true light now lights the spiritually minded, they live in the true world. In St. Paul's words, "They that are after the flesh do mind the things of the flesh; but they that are after the spirit the things of the spirit. For to be carnal minded is death; but to be spiritually minded is life and peace." But what is it to be spiritually minded, what world is that? The answer is clear: "Knowledge puffeth up, but love buildeth up." Those who still think they know do not know; they still live in the old world. "But if anyone love God the same is known of him" — love never fails, love alone overcomes sin and death. Prophecy, knowledge — these are partial states. Love alone is perfect, whole, complete.

Love that is without envy, without pride, that bears and suffers all things with joy, is more than *apatheia*. Detachment and purity have great qualities and accomplish much, but they do not compare with the living fire of love that can consume and transmute the sins of all worlds. Love is the active virtue, the only one able to realize the mystery of *identity* which, as the mystery of the Godhead, is also the mystery of the one true world. Therefore St. John writes, "Beloved, let us love one another: for love is of God; and everyone that loveth is born of God and knoweth God. He that loveth not God, knoweth not God; for *God is love*." And again: "He that dwelleth in love dwelleth in God, and God in him." For God so loved the world that he sent his only begotten Word into the world that we might live in him.

As Solovyov writes:

Having discerned in love the truth of another, not in the abstract but in substance, transferring in fact the center of our existence beyond the limits of the empiric personality, we reveal and make actual our own authentic truth, and our own absolute significance, which consists just in our capacity to transcend the limits of our actual phenomenal being, in our capacity to live not only in ourselves but in another.

Love one another, repeats St. John with childlike insistence. Affirm each other, be open to each other, wash each other's feet. Love each other as unconditionally and impersonally as God loved the world, the Word, his Son. Love without an object, as light to light, and the two worlds will become one.

7

St. Anthony said: Expect temptation with your last breath.

Bibliography

On Eriugena:

EDITIONS AND TRANSLATIONS:

Jeauneau, E. (ed) *Jean Scot: Commentaire sur L'Evangile de Jean,* Paris, 1972.
(ed) *Jean Scot: L'Homélie sur le Prologue de Jean,* Paris, 1969.
O'Meara (ed.), *Scot Erigène. Periphyseon (The Division of Nature)* tr. I-P. Sheldon-Williams, Paris, 1987.
Sheldon-Williams, I-P. (ed. & tr.) *Iohannis Scotti Eriugenae Periphyseon, Vols 1-III,* Dublin 1968.
Uhlfelder, M and Potter, *J. John the Scot, Periphyseon. On the Division of Nature,* Indianapolis, 1976.

STUDIES ETC.

Armstrong, A. H. *The Cambridge History of Later Greek and Early Medieval Philosophy,* Cambridge, 1970.
Beierwaltes, W. (ed.) *Eriugena Redivivus,* Heidelberg, 1987.
Bett, H. *Johannes Scotus Erigena: A Study in Medieval Philosophy,* London, 1925.
Cappuyns, M. *Jean Scot Erigene: Sa vie, son oeuvre, sa pensee,* Louvain, 1933.
Duclow, D. F. "Dialectic and Christology in Eriugena's Periphyseon." Dionysius 4 (1980).
"Divine Nothingness and Self-Creation in Johannes Scottus Eriugena." Journal of Religion 57 (1977).
Gardner, A. *Studies in John the Scot: A Philosopher of the Dark Ages,* Oxford, 1900.
Gersh, S. *From Iamblichus to Eriugena,* Leiden, 1978.
Jeauneau, E. *Quatres Themes erigeniens,* Montreal, 1978.
O'Meara, J. *Eriugena,* Cork, 1969.
Eriugena, Oxford, 1988.
O'Meara, J and Bieler, L (eds.) *The Mind of Eriugena,* Dublin, 1973.
Moran, D. *The Philosophy of John Scottus Eriugena: A Study of Idealism in the Middle Ages,* Cambridge, 1989.

Poole, R. L. *Illustrations of the History of Medieval Thought and Learning,* London, 1884 (reprinted New York, 1960).

Smalley, B. *The Study of the Bible in the Middle Ages,* Oxford, 1952.

Stock, B. "The Philosophical Anthropology of Johannes Scottus Eriugena." *Studi Medievali,* ser 3a, 8 (1967).

"Observations on the use of Augustine by Johannnes Scotus Eriugena." Harvard Theological Review 60 (1967).

Yates, F. A., "Ramon Lull and John Scotus Erigena." Journal of the Warburg and Courtauld Institutes 23 (1960).

BACKGROUND READING:

Allot, S. *Alcuin of York, AD 732-804: His Life and Letters,* New York, 1974.

Anderson, D. (trans.) *St. John of Damascus: On the Divine Images, Crestwood,* 1980.

Ante-Nicene Fathers, Volume X, (for Commentaries of Origen) Grand Rapids, 1978.

Bamberger, J. E. (trans.) *Evagrius Pontikus: The Praktikos; Chapters on Prayer,* Spencer, 1972

Barfield, O. *What Coleridge Thought,* Middletown, 1971.

Berdyaev, N. *The Meaning of the Creative Act,* New York, n.d.
The Destiny of Man, London, 1948.
Freedom and the Spirit, New York, 1935.

Berthold, G. C. (trans.) *Maximus Confessor: Selected Writings,* New York, 1985.

Bettenson, H. *The Early Christian Fathers,* Oxford, 1956.

Bieler L. *Ireland, Harbinger of the Middle Ages,* Oxford, 1966.

Blakney, R. B. *Meister Eckhart,* New York, 1941.

Brown, R. *The Community of the Beloved Disciple,* New York, 1979.

Bulgakov, S. *Le Paraclet,* Paris, 1946
The Wisdom of God, New York and London, n.d.

Butterworth, G. W. *Origen: On First Principles,* Gloucester, 1973.

Chadwick, N. *Studies in the Early British Church,* Cambridge, 1958.
The Age of Saints in the Celtic Church, Oxford, 1961.

Charlesworth J. H. (ed.) *John and Qumran,* London, 1972.

Chitty, D. (tr.) *Letters of Saint Antony the Great,* Oxford, 1975.

Colledge, E. (trans.) *Meister Eckhart: The Essential Sermons, Commentaries, Treatises etc.,* New York, 1981.

Corbin, H. *Avicenna and the Visionary Recital,* Dallas, 1980.
Creative Imagination in the Sufism of Ibn Arabi, Princeton, 1969.

Dillon, J. *The Middle Platonists,* London, 1977.

Deck, J. *Nature, Contemplation and the One,* Toronto, 1967.

Dodds E. R. (ed.) *Proclus: the Elements of Theology,* Oxford, 1963.

Florensky, P. *La Colonne et le Fondement de la Verite,* Lausanne, 1975

Florovsky, G. *Aspects of Church History,* Belmont, Mass., 1975.

Foerster, W. *Gnosis: A Selection of Texts, Vol. 1,* Oxford, 1972.

Frank, S. L. *Reality and Man,* New York, 1965.

Fulcanelli, *The Mystery of the Cathedrals,* London, 1971.

Gendle, N. (trans.) *Gregory Palamas: The Triads,* New York, 1983.

Gilson, E. *A History of Christian Philosophy in the Middle Ages,* New York, 1955.

The Christian Philosophy of St. Augustine, New York, 1960.

Gougaud, L. *Christianity in Celtic Lands,* London, 1932.

Hamilton, E. and Cairns, H. *The Collected Dialogues of Plato,* Princeton, 1973.

Hanson, W. G. *The Early Monastic Schools of Ireland,* Cambridge, 1927.

Hardy E. R. (ed.) *Christology of the Later Fathers,* Philaldephia, 1954.

Hathaway, R. F. *Hierarchy and the Definition of Order in the Letters of Pseudo-Dionysius,* The Hague, 1969.

Heidegger M. *Discourse on Thinking,* New York, 1966.

Identity and Difference, New York, 1969.

Hughes, K. *Early Christian Ireland,* Cambridge, 1979.

Inge, W. R. *The Philosophy of Plotinus,* London, 1929.

John XXIII Lectures, New York, 1966.

Kühlewind, G. *Becoming Aware of the Logos,* West Stockbridge, 1985.

Ladner, G. B. *The Idea of Reform,* New York, 1967.

Laistner, M. L. W. *Thought and Letters in Western Europe A.D. 500-900,* Ithaca, 1958.

Leff, G. *Heresy in the Later Middle Ages,* Manchester, 1967.

Lonergan, B. *The Way to Nicea,* Philadelphia, 1976.

Lossky, V. *The Vision of God,* London, 1963.

The Mystical Theology of the Eastern Church, London, 1957.

On the Image and Likeness of God, Crestwood, 1974.

Orthodox Theology, Crestwood, 1978.

Lubheid, C. (trans.) *Pseudo-Dionysius: The Complete Works,* New York, 1987.

McCool, G. A. *A Rahner Reader,* New York, 1981

McGinn, B. (ed.) *Meister Eckhart: Teacher and Preacher,* New York, 1986.

McKenna, S. (trans.) *Plotinus. The Enneads,* London, 1969.

Macleod, F, *The Divine Adventure: Iona,* New York, 1910.

Manteau-Bonamy, H. M. *Immaculate Conception and the Holy Spirit: The Marian Teachings of Father Kolbe,* Liberyville, 1977.

Mantzaridis, G. *The Deification of Man,* Crestwood, 1984.

Massignham, H. J. *The Tree of Life,* London, 1943.

Maurer, A. (trans.) *Meister Eckhart: Parisian Questions and Prologues,* Toronto, 1974.

Mead, G. R. S. *Thrice Greatest Hermes,* London, 1964.

Meyendorff, J. *A Study of Gregory Palamas,* Crestood, 1974.
   St. Gregory Palamas and Orthodox Spirituality, Crestwood, 1974.
   Christ in Eastern Christian Thought, Crestwood, 1975.

Moltmann, J. *The Trinity and the Kingdom,* New York, 1981.

Merlan, P. *From Platonism to Neoplatonism,* The Hague, 1960.
   Monopsychism, Mysticism, Metaconsciousness, The Hague, 1963.

Merton, T. (trans) *Clement of Alexandria: Selections from The Protreptikos,* New York, 1962.

Mueller, B. *Goethe's Botanical Writings,* Honolulu, 1952.

Nash, R. H. *The Light of Mind: St. Augustine's Theory of Knowledge,* Lexington, 1969.

Needleman, J. *Lost Christianity,* New York, 1980.

The Nicene and Post-Nicene Fathers, Volumes VIII (Basil) and X (Gregory of Nyssa), Grand Rapids, 1978.

Oates, W. J. (ed.) *St. Augustine: Basic Writings,* New York, 1948.

O'Meara J. J. (trans.) *Origen: Prayer; Exhortation to Martyrdom,* New York, 1954.

Pagels, E. *The Johannine Gospel in Gnostic Exegesis,* Nashville and New York, 1973.
   The Gnostic Paul, Philadelphia, 1975.

Payne, R. *The Holy Fire: The Story of the Fathers of the Eastern Church,* London, 1958.

Pannikar, R. *The Trinity and the Religious Experience of Man,* New York, 1973.

Pelikan, J. *The Christian Tradition, three volumes,* Chicago, 1971. 1974, 1978.

Pennington, M. P. (ed.) *One Yet Two: Monastic Tradition East and West,* Kalamazoo, 1976.

Prestige, G. L. *Fathers and Heretics,* London, 1977.
   God in Patristic Thought, London, 1952.

Rahner, H. *Greek Myths and Christian Mystery,* New York, 1963.

Rahner, K. *Foundations of Christian Faith,* New York, 1978.

Ricoeur, P. *The Symbolism of Evil,* Boston, 1969.

Essays on Biblical Interpretation, Philadelphia, 1980.

Rist, J. M. *Plotinus: The Road to Reality,* Cambridge, 1967.

Eros and Psyche: Studies in Plato, Plotinus and Origen, Toronto, 1964.

Robinson, J. A. T. *The Body: A Study in Pauline Thought,* Philadelphia, n.d.

Robinson, J. M. (ed) *The Nag Hammadi Library,* New York, 1977.

Rosenstock-Huessy, E. *Speech and Reality,* Norwich, Vermont, 1970.

The Fruit of Lips or Why Four Gospels, Pittsburgh, 1978.

Schurmann, R. *Meister Eckhart: Mystic and Philosopher,* Bloomington, 1978.

Schwaller de Lubicz, R. A. *Nature Word,* West Stockbridge, 1982.

Esotericism and Symbol, New York, 1985.

Le Temple de l'Homme, Lyon, 1957.

Scott, W. (trans.) *Hermetica,* Boulder, 1982.

Sherwood, P. *The Earlier Ambigua of Maximus the Confessor and his Refutation of Origenism,* Rome, 1955.

(trans.) *St Maximus the Confessor: The Ascetic Life; The Four Centuries on Charity,* New York, 1955.

Solovyov, V. *The Meaning of Love,* West Stockbridge, 1987.

Stahl, W. H (et al) (eds) *Martianus Capella and the Seven Liberal Arts, Two vols,* New York, 1971 and 1978.

Stead, C. *Divine Substance,* Oxford, 1977.

Steiner, R. *Christianity as Mystical Fact,* New York, 1976.

The Gospel of St. John, New York, 1973.

Building Stones for an Understanding of the Mystery of Golgotha, London, 1972.

From Jesus to Christ, London, 1973.

Mystery Knowledge and Mystery Centers, London, 1973.

The Inner Realities of Evolution, London,

The Redemption of Thinking, New York, 1983.

Swedenborg, E. *The Divine Love and Wisdom,* London, 1912.

Taylor, M. J. *A Companion to John,* New York, 1977.

Tollinton, R. B. *Alexandrine Teaching on the Universe,* New York, 1932.

Thunberg, L. *Man and Cosmos: The Vision of Maximus the Confessor,* Crestwood, 1985.

Microcosm and Mediator: The Theological Anthropology of Maximus the Confessor, Lund, 1965.

Von Balthasar, H. U. *Liturgie Cosmique,* Paris, 1947.
    The Glory of the Lord, volume 1, San Francisco, 1982
Weill, S. *Intimations of Christianity Among the Ancient Greeks,* London 1957.
    The Notebooks of Simone Weill, New York, 1956.
    Science, Necessity and the Love of God, Oxford, 1968.
Wallis, R. T. *The Neoplatonists,* London, 1972.
Ward, B. (trans.) *Sayings of the Desert Fathers,* Kalamazoo, 1975.
Zernov, N., and Pain, J. *A Bulgakov Anthology,* Philadelphia 1976
Zouboff, P. P. *Soloviev on Godmanhood,* New York, 1946